101
Easy
WAYS
TO MAKE YOUR
HOME SELL
FASTER

101 Easy WAYS TO MAKE YOUR HOME SELL FASTER

by Barbara Jane Hall

FAWCETT COLUMBINE • NEW YORK

A Fawcett Columbine Book
Published by Ballantine Books

Library of Congress Catalog Card Number: 84-91675
ISBN 0-449-90145-9

Design by Holly Johnson at the Angelica Design Group, Ltd.
Cover design by James R. Harris
Manufactured in the United States of America
First Edition: April 1985
10 9 8 7 6 5 4 3 2 1

Contents

Why is it that one house sells within days after the realtor's sign appears on the front lawn and another lingers for months on the market? You've probably seen this happen in your own neighborhood: the Harrisons' charming little Cape sells the first week for the full asking price while the Campbells' tidy Colonial languishes for seven months before it finally moves at $8,000 less than the listed price.

In today's tough real estate market, far too many sellers are spending endless months, even years, watching prospective buyers troop through their homes without making an offer. To avoid this kind of frustration, you must learn the secrets of making your house more salable. And no, you needn't invest $5,000 in a new redwood deck or $10,000 in an in-ground swimming pool to make your home a quick seller. The fact is, if you were to carry out all 101 tips recommended in this book, your total outlay would be measured in mere hundreds rather than thousands of dollars.

That's right, most of the following 101 tips will cost you little or nothing. If you want to reap the rewards of a fast sale of your home, what you must be willing to invest are your time, your imagination, and a little old-fashioned elbow grease.

The rewards should be obvious to all. There may, of course, be urgent reasons why you have to move, such as a job transfer, relocation, or retirement. Ask any friend or neighbor whose house took ages to sell, and you will hear an all too common tale of frustration, annoyance, inconvenience, and disappointment. Having hordes of strangers invading your private domain for months on end is no picnic for you and your family.

More important is the fact that the longer a house is on the market, the less likely the seller is to receive a high offer. It's human nature to suspect the quality of merchandise that has been "on the shelf" for a long time. A slow-selling house makes prospective buyers nervous. More often than not they either reject the house or make a ridiculously low offer in the hope and belief that the weary and discouraged owner is desperate to sell.

Happily, it doesn't have to be this way. Selling your home, though rarely a "fun" experience, can be a painless and profitable one—if you follow the guidelines offered on the following pages. And don't neglect to involve your family in this project. It is a cooperative venture with one shared goal: to make your home sell fast.

Part 1

THE GROUNDWORK

Understand what you're selling.

Remember that you're not selling a house, you're selling a *home*. That structure consists of far more than four walls and a roof. A home is a personal shelter, a haven from the pressures of the outside world, and a warm, inviting setting for family living. Although a house is probably the biggest purchase a couple ever makes, the decision to buy one is never purely rational. Buyers buy with their heads *and* their hearts.

Beyond the obvious considerations of location, size, quality of construction, present condition, and design, buyers look for special qualities that appeal to their emotions. Often they probably have no idea what these hidden, emotional qualities are that draw them to one house over another. *It's your job to prepare the groundwork, to set the scene for a buyer to fall in love with your home.* Believe it or not, many a house has sold quickly because of a spectacular lilac bush, a cozy windowseat tucked under the eaves, or a kitchen bay window filled with potted herbs.

Put yourself in the buyers' shoes, and remember that they arrive at your front door *wanting* to fall in love with your home. They are eager and filled with happy expectations. If you don't know how to take advantage of these feelings, your customer is likely to beat a hasty retreat with a tight smile and a "thank you very much." On the other hand, if you've done your homework and set the stage, or stages, correctly, every room in your home will greet the customer with a pleasant surprise. Your home will sell itself.

What makes your home special?

Let us assume that you and your family have made the big decision. You're ready to sell. You're no longer just thinking about it or toying with the idea. This is the real thing. First, settle down in your favorite easy chair, close your eyes, and try to remember your feelings the very first time *you* walked into your home. Now, pick up a pencil and start listing your impressions of your home's most positive features in the first column of Chart One (opposite). This list should be purely subjective. Let your remembered feelings be your guide: the more personal, the better.

Ask your spouse and your children to add their own special positive reactions to the chart. Don't forget that it's important to get a "child's-eye view" if you hope to sell to another family with children. Your teenage daughter may remember how she fell in love with your home years ago because of a swing that hung from the old oak tree in your backyard. Don't make the mistake of ignoring children's special impressions. They are an invaluable addition to this chart.

To complete the list, take a slow tour through every room in the house (bathrooms, too), then canvas the attic, basement, garage, and finally the yard. Make an effort to note at least one positive feature in each area. Include not only the items that attracted you to the house in the first place, but also those desirable features you have added since you bought it. If your list spills off the printed chart, as it probably will, lucky you! You've discovered that your home has lots of salable assets.

No home is perfect, even yours.

This exercise is tougher, but equally important. Your first list was fun; for this one, you have to be ruthless. Try to imagine that you are a stranger seeing your own house for the first time. Plunge right into the spirit of the game by starting your dispassionate tour from the street. Then take a pencil and start filling in the first column of Chart Two (page 6) with every negative feature you can find.

Don't skip any area of your home or property. Is the upstairs hall too long and dark? Is the kitchen too small? Is that forsythia bush getting out of hand? Again, invite your family to participate. Try not to let your love for your home color your objectivity.

You must neither close your eyes to your home's negative features nor let them depress you. Once aware of them, you're going to learn to solve the problems with ingenuity—and a very small outlay of cash, if any.

Chart One: Our home's best selling features

Positive Features	How to highlight them

Chart Two: Our home's selling drawbacks

Negative Features	How to transform them

Accentuate the positive.

A real estate agent may bring prospective buyers to your door, but don't rely on him or her to do the whole job of selling your home. A salable home speaks for itself, each room sending out a unique message to the customer. It is far more effective to have buyers "discover" your home's special features themselves than to have the owner or agent point them out like a tour guide.

Short of installing neon signs in every room, how can you draw attention to your home's best assets? All it takes is a little creativity: a cheerful glow of logs in the fireplace; a spotlight beaming down on the gameboard set up in your family room; a pot of red geraniums by your front door.

Take the example of your teenager who remembered falling in love with your home because of a swing hanging from the old oak tree. You listed that tree as a plus; now accentuate it as a selling point. Buyers will notice that tree if you hang the swing there again, if you group two or three lawn chairs in its inviting shade, or replace the sparsely growing grass around its trunk with a bed of vivid red impatiens. *Stimulate the customers' imaginations by setting the scene for them.* If you can draw them into that scene and make them see themselves living happily ever after there, they will already be halfway toward making an offer for your house.

Now, start filling in the second column of Chart One with ways and means of visually highlighting each of your home's best assets. Don't worry if immediate solutions do not leap to mind. This book is filled with suggestions for drawing the buyers' attention to your home's most attractive selling points.

Eliminate the negative.

You can eliminate many of your home's negative features by transforming them into something more visually pleasant. Clever disguises may not turn a sow's ear into a silk purse, but there are many cheap and creative solutions to problem areas that will minimize, if not eliminate, those drawbacks.

A long, dark hall, for instance, will appear shorter if it's wallpapered in vertical pastel stripes. By hanging a few pictures (borrow them from other rooms) on the walls and installing inexpensive gallery lights above them, you will stop the buyers' eyes along the way and the monotonous tunnel effect will be eliminated.

It's time now to start filling in the second column of Chart Two. But don't despair if you can't come up with obvious answers to every problem. After you read the following 101 tips, you'll be thinking more creatively and you'll be ready to tackle—and conquer—any difficult area of your home.

An educated seller is an effective seller.

Setting the proper stage is perhaps three-quarters of the battle. Once you've highlighted your home's selling strengths and masked its weaknesses, however, you've still got to locate the right buyer. How to go about it?

In a number of ways. For one, your chances of selling *quickly* —which is what this book is all about—are usually improved by employing the services of an experienced real estate agent. If it is true that a lawyer who represents himself has a fool for a client, is it not also true of the home-owner who tries to sell his own home?

If you're a wise seller, you will make your home more salable *before* contacting an agent. Agents are human beings, after all, with the same emotional responses as buyers. They will work more diligently for you if you've convinced them that your house is ready to sell.

It's possible to sell without an agent, of course, but it is the rare individual who can provide the same skill that an agent can bring to the job of selling a house. Why? Because the agent has the know-how and selling experience that you probably lack. Because the agent has the backup of an ongoing organization that can effectively advertise and promote your home to potential customers. Because the agent already has an active list of customers who may be predisposed to buy your home. And because the agent's expertise will lead you to a proper determination of the selling price that will make your home sell quickly to a qualified buyer.

Before you rush to the phone, however, you should study the tips in this book on choosing an agent. Learn what you can and *should* expect from an agent. Learn how to interview an agent before listing your home. And learn how to deal most effectively with agent *and* customer when they inspect your home.

In other words, educate yourself, and then deal from a position of strength, with both agent and buyer, in selling your home. Why take chances with your most cherished and valuable possession?

Part 2

101 TIPS

GENERAL CONSIDERATIONS

1. Make those minor repairs.

Like most home-owners, you've probably stayed on top of major repairs and maintenance, making sure that your house is painted regularly, that your furnace is running efficiently, that your roof isn't leaking. It's those *minor* tasks that seem to get neglected for months on end—that leaky bathroom faucet, that broken doorbell, that torn window screen in the bedroom. Yes, the faucet sometimes rivals the Chinese water torture in the still of the night, the doorbell sounds as if it's ringing in Outer Mongolia, and that tiny hole in the screen seems to let in some remarkably large mosquitoes; but somehow there is always something more urgent to do. *Mañana*, you say, I'll fix it tomorrow.

Well, sellers, *mañana* has come! All those tiny little flaws in your otherwise beautifully maintained home will add up to one thing to the observant buyer: the dreaded O.N., otherwise known as Owner Neglect. If you want to sell your home quickly for a good price (and who doesn't?), all signs of Owner Neglect must be eliminated. Your only recourse is to arm yourself with pad and pencil and launch an immediate, super-critical tour of your home, inside and out. Note all such offenders as loose doorknobs, cracked window panes, peeling paint, creaking hinges, sluggish drains, rusting gutters, crumbling grout, etc.

Don't shrug and count on buyers to overlook these seemingly minor imperfections. Maybe you've lived with that Inner Sanctum basement door for five years, but you can't be sure it won't scare the living daylights out of a prospective buyer. Will that buyer be impressed with the size of your master bedroom if the doorknob falls off in his hand, the window sash sticks, and the overhead light fails to illuminate this beautiful room when you flip the switch?

It's annoying little flaws like these that keep your home from showing its best and often add up to a no-sale for you and your family. Need one say more? Get thee to a hardware store, and then make those minor repairs!

2. Regardless of season, tackle spring cleaning.

A bright, well-scrubbed home not only will sell faster than a dull, dingy one, it may sell for a considerably higher price. Dreary though they may be, those hours spent thoroughly cleaning your home will be hours well spent when the result pays off in an early and profitable sale.

An old-fashioned spring cleaning is a top-to-bottom job, not a superficial slap of the dust rag to remove cobwebs. Maybe Granny did it only in the spring, but if you have to sell your home in the dead of winter, that is the time to tackle the job. Involve everyone in the family; assign tasks in a very systematic way. Or hire some energetic teenagers who have more pizzaz than you do. Or, if you can afford it, employ a professional cleaning service. Just be sure you get this all-important job done, and don't miss a corner. Clean out every closet, every cupboard, every nook and cranny. Remember, if you hope to sell your home for top dollar, it must be spotless.

You'd be surprised how many sellers neglect to clean their windows when in fact this chore should be at the top of everyone's list. In certain lights, dirty windows can be noticed from the street, and will certainly create a poor first impression as buyers approach your home. Your entire house will appear brighter and sunnier, even on a gloomy day, if your windows sparkle.

You should also pay particular attention to your kitchen and bathrooms when doing this spring cleaning. Because they involve personal health and hygiene, these are areas that buyers particularly expect to gleam. Of course, vinyl floors should shine, appliances sparkle. But don't neglect to clean out kitchen cupboards and lay in fresh shelf liner; you never know who is going to poke around in there. Toss out those year-old, half filled boxes of cereal and any other food you're never going to use. Crowded cupboards will only suggest to the buyer that your kitchen storage space is inadequate. And while you're at it, weed out plates, pots, pans, and glasses that you don't need. (They can be reserved for the yard sale you'll learn about in the next tip.)

Don't duck the big tasks. Do your wood floors need waxing? Does your wall-to-wall carpeting need a good cleaning? Are your curtains and draperies dirty and lifeless? Be honest—and make your home reflect true pride of ownership.

Once you have your home in tip-top shape, you must try to keep it that way so that you'll be prepared for showings at any time. For a large family, this can be a tough proposition, but you can manage it if you're well organized. Enlist your entire family's cooperation in keeping your home showroom-clean during this all-important period while your house is on the market.

3. Have a yard sale before you list your home.

Most owners wait until their houses have sold before having a yard sale, but this is usually a mistake. Unless you belong to that select club of neat, super-organized folks who regularly throw things out and save nothing they can't use, it's an excellent idea to have a yard sale before you even think of calling a real estate agent.

During your spring cleaning, you surely found piles of outgrown clothes, boxes of dishes you never use, old bedspreads, draperies, etc. If you sell all of this useless clutter now, your home will look neater and therefore more attractive, your storage areas will look more spacious, and you can earn a little money to finance some of the other inexpensive projects suggested in this book for making your home more salable.

Some yard sale pointers:

—Make it a joint sale with a neighbor. It's more fun to share the headaches and humor of the event with a friend, and when those eager buyers descend like birds of prey, it's good to have all the assistance you can get. Also, by pooling your efforts with a neighbor, you'll double the size of the yard sale, which will probably draw far more buyers.

—Advertise in local papers, and be sure to list some specific "goodies" to attract buyers. If you have old Depression glass to sell, say so; it sounds much more inviting than just a vague reference to "household items."

—How many times have you swerved and nearly cracked into a telephone pole trying to figure out where somebody's yard sale is? Make a lot of large, *readable* signs with clear directions to your sale, and post them all around town.

—Price your items realistically and expect to barter. There's just no point in holding out for another quarter if someone doesn't quite meet your price. And if something doesn't sell early in the day, don't hesitate to mark down the price for the latecomers. Keep remembering that your goal is to get rid of the stuff.

—What doesn't sell goes to the Salvation Army or to your church bazaar, *not* back into your house. If charity won't take your leftovers, head for the nearest dump, where they should have been deposited long ago.

4. Create the illusion of spaciousness.

Most buyers are looking for space, as large a living space as their money can buy. During the recent years of skyrocketing construction costs, buyers have had to settle for smaller and smaller homes, yet they still want their rooms to give a large appearance.

Even if you think your rooms are adequately sized, make your living space *appear* as large as possible by eliminating bulky, unnecessary furniture. Sell it, store it, or give it away—anything to get it out of sight while you are trying to make your rooms look open and spacious. You can sell furniture at your yard sale, you can store it with a sympathetic neighbor, or you can donate it to charity and take a tax deduction. Whatever it takes, open up your rooms for potential buyers; make it possible for them to imagine living comfortably, breathing easy in these spaces.

For example, is your "master" bedroom pathetically small? Give some thought to making the room seem larger by storing one of your two bureaus in the attic. You and your mate can always consolidate your clothes for a month or two. Giving the room a larger appearance is well worth the relatively minor inconvenience.

Another example: consider rearranging furniture to give the illusion of spaciousness. Even though you've enjoyed your couch positioned in the middle of the living room in front of the fireplace, the room will probably look much larger if you place the couch against a wall. Move your furniture around. Experiment.

Check your walls and be sure you don't have too many pictures, which can make a room seem smaller than it is. Are your windows too crowded with hanging plants? You may love them yourself, but half as many will let in twice the light and open up your space.

If all else fails, remember the old mirror trick. A large, well-placed mirror can give the illusion of doubling the space. Use them with some discretion, of course, or your home could wind up looking like an amusement park hall of mirrors.

5. Give your rooms a light, bright look.

When asked about their ideal house, most buyers respond that they want large, bright, cheerful rooms. If your home has a lot of windows, you have a treasure, but you should capitalize on that asset by removing heavy draperies that hide the sun. Keep window shades rolled up and Venetian blinds open and let the sun shine in. Check shrubbery and trees outside first-floor windows to be sure light is not being cut off by overgrown foliage. Light is equated with cheerfulness, and a cheerful customer is one who is more likely to respond positively to your home by pulling out his checkbook.

If your home has a very bright sunny room, you have another treasure. Emphasize this great asset by hanging a plant or two in the windows. (Not *too* many plants, as noted in the last tip.) Try an easy, ever-flowering plant like wax begonia, which loves the sun, or, in season, a Christmas cactus. You don't have to have a green thumb to keep them alive for the short time you will be showing your home. Just buy a couple of full, fresh plants, water them twice a week, and smile when prospective buyers compliment you on your spectacular *Schlumbergeras*.

Almost every home has a dark room or two, where the sun never seems to shine. Be absolutely sure that these rooms are not painted a dark color. It's quite easy and inexpensive to get rid of that cavelike feeling with a couple of coats of white or pastel paint. Be sure the curtains are sheer, and increase the wattage of the light bulbs in these darker rooms. You may love the coziness of your tiny, navy-blue spare bedroom, but don't count on most buyers to share your feelings. They may well have trouble picturing it as a pale pink nursery for their baby girl.

6. Use color and lighting to draw attention to your home's bestselling features.

Bright colors demand attention. In a room decorated in somber earth tones, a flaming orange pillow will be the first thing you notice. Against a wall of white shutters, a cobalt-blue vase filed with anemones silently shouts, "Look at me!" As an educated seller, you should learn to use this powerful, magnetic quality of color as an effective selling tool.

Do you want to direct the buyer's eye toward that charming little windowseat in the master bedroom? Simply arrange some brightly colored pillows in the corner, or fold a boldly patterned quilt on the bench. This colorfully positive feature thus becomes a focal point of the room, leading the buyer to respond, "How inviting!"

Don't expect buyers to notice your home's best selling features without a little help on your part. Highlight the graceful bay window in your living room by placing a colorful arrangement of flowers on a table in front of the window. If a brick-paved patio is your pride and joy, buy a bright checkered tablecloth for your redwood table to draw the buyer's eye to this area. Or consider purchasing that cheerful striped table umbrella that you've been coveting. (To be sure, umbrellas can be costly, but you can always take one with you after it's helped sell your home.)

Color has power to attract, but do use some restraint. A riot of color can prove distracting to a buyer. You should use color selectively to accent a particular area, to draw the buyer's attention to one special thing at a time.

Lighting should also be used for emphasis. For example, you can effectively draw attention to a handsome wall of bookcases by placing a few small accent lamps in random pattern on the shelves. Or consider spotlighting the detailed carving of your ceiling's molding with a well-placed lamp. If you have track lights, let them shine down on your prized oak parquet floors. Gallery lights are relatively inexpensive and can be used to great effect to highlight a special painting. Not that you're going to leave the artwork behind, but emphasizing it in this manner can only contribute to the special charm and ambience of your home, and suggest to the buyer that he, too, can create the same look when your home is his.

7. Disguise unsightly views.

If you have this problem, closing your curtains or drapes may only advertise the fact that you are trying to hide a less-than-picture-perfect view. Out of curiosity, if nothing else, many a buyer will automatically make a beeline to those heavy draperies to see for himself what lurks beyond. On the other hand, you may have become so accustomed to the sight of your neighbor's wash-line that you expect a prospective buyer to ignore such an unsightly view from your window.

But why worry about a buyer's negative reaction when you can easily and inexpensively disguise the potentially offending vista? Whatever solution you choose, remember that it's important always to let light into your rooms. Some possibilities:

—Remove heavy curtains and install a panel of white-painted latticework cut and fitted to your window opening. In front of the lattice, hang a feathery asparagus fern, which will not block much light. Presto! Just as a magician distracts your eye while he practices his sleight of hand, you will hide your unsightly view in a most charming way.

—Replace heavy curtains with sheer white panels that will cover the window and yet let in plenty of light. Also, experiment with pretty curtain treatments *around* the window. A few yards of glossy chintz fabric will draw the eye away from the view.

—Interior window shutters are not cheap, but they certainly do the job if you want to hide your view. If you're trying to make the town dump disappear, the expense of interior shutters may pay off. In any case, be certain that the louvres are tilted to let in enough light. Similarly, if your home is contemporary in style, you might consider screening an offensive view with attractive vertical blinds, which can be adjusted to let in sufficient light while at the same time obscuring your neighbor's trash cans.

—Consider installing three or four glass shelves in the problem window, then filling them with pretty colored glass bottles. They needn't be valuable antiques; you can find lovely cheap ones at yard sales and flea markets. Your room will look bright and cheerful, and the buyer's eye will be captivated by the bottle collection rather than dismayed by the view beyond.

Above all, don't apologize for a poor view. Never mention it to a salesperson or a buyer. Instead, take pride in your cleverness at being able to turn your liability into an asset that will help rather than hinder the sale of your home.

8. Eliminate unpleasant odors.

No matter how beautiful your home is to behold, it must also
smell good—i.e., clean. Remember that some people are much
more sensitive to odors than others. Smokers rarely notice the
stench of tobacco that fills their homes, and pet owners may be
oblivious to objectionable doggy odor. You cannot assume, however, that your house-buying customers will be among those with
deadened olfactory facilities.

Go outdoors and take several deep breaths of fresh air, then
embark on a sniffing tour of your home, and be consciously on
the lookout (smellout?) for offensive odors. If your den reeks of
stale cigarette smoke, vacuum the draperies and rugs that hold
these odors, or send them out for professional cleaning if that
doesn't work. If your pets have made mistakes on rugs and carpeting, clean that odor out; powdered products like "Love My
Carpet" are quite effective. Be sure to tuck litter boxes into obscure corners and remember to change the litter frequently (use
the deodorized brands).

Obviously, your kitchen should not reek of grease and garbage.
If your stove has no exhaust system, buy an inexpensive air puri-
fier for the room and turn it on whenever you're cooking. Some
of these products actually counter bad odors with a pleasant
lemon scent. Trash cans and diaper pails should be cleaned frequently with a strong disinfectant and fitted with deodorizing
tablets that attach to the inside of the lid.

Mildew odors in basements and bathrooms are another no-no,
and must be eliminated by scrubbing and spraying with products
such as Lysol. Don't allow wet towels to accumulate in hampers,
or old laundry to pile up in closets, which can soon begin to smell
like gymnasium lockers. Weed out the sources of the offending
odors and hang bags of cedar chips in closets for a pleasant smell.
Potpourris and sachets throughout the house are also very helpful in creating an appealingly fresh-scented environment.

9. Avoid eccentricities.

Your chances of selling quickly will be greatly improved if you
can make your home appeal to a broad spectrum of buyers. It
may be tempting to say of your home, "But this is *me!*" but this is
not necessarily a wise home-selling policy. The smart seller will
try to play down those very individualistic touches that may ex-

press perfectly his taste and personality but, at the same time, may appeal to a very small minority of home buyers. After all, if you had intended simply to relax in your beanbag chair, meditate before your Pink Floyd poster, light some incense, and wait for a well-heeled hippy to buy your pad, you probably wouldn't be reading this book in the first place.

In the game of selling, you have to play the odds. If your rooms are painted purple and beaded curtains hang in every doorway, don't rely on your real estate agent to find the perfect buyer whose gypsy tastes match yours. The average buyer will have a hard time looking beyond purple walls and eccentric decor. Two coats of white paint may be the best investment you ever made— and of course you can always revert to purple and beads in your next home.

If your bedroom was designed by Hugh Hefner, the mirrored walls and ceilings may make some prospective buyers quite uncomfortable. Consider playing down the "pleasure palace" look while your house is on the market in order to avoid needlessly offending people.

Other areas of possible offense are those two old bugaboos, politics and religion. Everyone is entitled to his own beliefs in these areas, but if you are trying to sell to the widest possible market—and you should be—it is not wise to make your living room look like campaign headquarters or your dining room resemble a sacred temple.

10. Recognize the fine line between clutter and sterility.

Take a few minutes to study the photographs in your favorite home-decorating magazines. Notice the small details that make the rooms particularly attractive and appealing—a vase of flowers, an open book on the coffee table, a brightly colored pillow in a wing chair, a basket of knitting yarns. Take a tip from the professionals who set up these pictures: accessories can make or break a room. Too many discordant elements in a room can make the area look small and "busy," yet a room without personal accessories will appear as cold and antiseptic as a furniture showroom.

There are people who love clutter and there are people who enjoy stark simplicity in their lifestyles. Most, however, prefer a harmonious balance between the two extremes. Since you are trying to make your home appeal to as many prospective buyers as possible, you should check your decor with an impersonal eye and try to see it as a stranger might.

Try this exercise: Imagine that *House Beautiful* is going to feature your home in an upcoming issue and you're to be the photographer's assistant. Find an old shirt cardboard and cut out a rectangular opening approximately 2" x 3". Studying your familiar rooms through this makeshift viewfinder will force you to concentrate on one area at a time. This process will refine your field of vision and should help you to see your rooms from a fresh perspective.

Stand in the doorway of each room, look through your cardboard frame, and study the picture. Should you add anything to the scene? Does the room need a spot of color, an item of interest? For instance, suppose your bureau top looks bare. Why not move the dried flowers from the dining room into the bedroom? On the bureau top with the mirror behind them, they might be just the thing to counter the sterile look you're trying to avoid.

As you tour your home in this fashion, be on the lookout for distracting clutter. Hundreds of framed family photographs displayed on table tops, windowsills, bookshelves, and television consoles are sure to divert a prospective buyer's attention from the pleasant proportions or other fine features of the room. Until your house is sold, pack Aunt Bessie and Uncle Albie away in the back of the closet.

The same advice holds true for hobbies and collections. A beautiful amethyst geode displayed and spotlighted on the mantle can be lovely, but dozens of them glittering from every available flat surface in the room would be clutter to anyone but the serious rockhound. And just how many of your prospective buyers will be serious rockhounds?

11. Display photographs that show your home during other seasons.

Not only is spring the most active home-buying season, it is probably the time of year when your home looks its very best. The lawn is lush and green; flowering trees are filling the fresh air with a heady aroma; daffodils, tulips, and violets are blooming. In such a setting, on a bright, sunny spring day, your home can seem absolutely irresistible to an eager buyer.

But what if you have to sell in the dead of winter? Will a buyer be able to imagine the three hundred naturalized daffodils that are now sleeping under a foot of snow? You may brag about the rare and expensive perennials that you've planted over the years, but, as the old saying goes, one picture is worth a thousand words.

Go through your photo albums and select pictures of your house and yard during all four seasons. These will be important selling tools. If you have a spectacular cutting garden, a rock garden, a rose garden, be sure to select pictures of these assets at their peak growing times. And be sure to include photographs of outdoor living spaces—patios, barbecue areas, and decks set up with summer furniture or a hammock stretched between two trees.

Round out your selection of seasonal photographs with one of your home at Christmas with a wreath on the door or a snowman in the front yard, or choose a picture of that beautiful maple tree in the front yard wearing its bright red fall leaves. One word of caution: in selecting these representative photographs, don't include your favorite Blizzard of '67 shot of the drifted snow halfway up your chimney. The same goes for that picture of your kids frolicking in six-foot-high piles of autumn leaves. It's best not to remind a prospective home buyer of the "joys" of shoveling and raking.

Once you have narrowed your selection of photographs, arrange them on an inexpensive cork bulletin board, which you can hang in the kitchen or family room. Don't offend buyers with unnecessary cute little captions. If the board is hung at eye level in a well-lighted area, the pictures will speak for themselves and give you yet another selling edge.

FRONT DOOR AND PORCH

First impressions are indelible. No matter how lovely your home may be behind that front door, a buyer will be turned off by crumbling front steps, a doorbell that doesn't work, creaky hinges, or chipping paint on porch columns. Confronted by such immediate problems, he will then tour your home with a negative attitude and need a lot of convincing to overcome his initial reaction.

So give special attention to your home's front entry. Polish the door knocker until it gleams, scrub all traces of moss or mildew from the brick steps, touch up any peeling paint. As always, put yourself in the buyer's place and build up his expectations as he waits to enter. Remember, his first impression is likely to color the remainder of the house tour.

12. Create a welcoming spot of color.

When a prospective buyer pulls up in front of your home, there should be something special that beckons him toward your front door, something that sets your home off from the other houses on the block. This is particularly true if your home is cut from a standard ranch, split-level, or Colonial mold.

Take the case of a young couple who restored a small, rather ordinary farmhouse, then placed a bright red milk can on their porch beside the front door. That cheery touch of color makes the little house special. Never mind that the house itself is homely; the milk can creates a warm and welcoming first impression.

You can accomplish the same goal with a tub of geraniums, a pot of floppy petunias, or a basket of nasturtiums. In the winter, your home needs a touch of welcoming color more than ever. Consider painting a child's old sled a bright red or green and propping it beside your front door.

Perhaps the easiest way to add color to your home is to paint the front door itself. Choose a color that harmonizes with the existing color of your home—for instance, if your siding is weathered cedar shakes, wedgwood blue is a lovely accent color; brick red might be the perfect door color if your home is painted an earthy brown; if your house is white, try a forest green.

Needless to say, avoid odd and off-putting colors like shocking pink or chartreuse, which appeal only to a few. Color can be a psychological pull; use it to attract your buyers in the most positive way you can.

13. Invest in a new doormat.

Obvious? You'd be surprised how few sellers think of making this simple purchase. An old, worn doormat serves no purpose at all other than to give the buyer a poor first impression of your home. With countless people trooping through your home in the next few weeks, you'll be glad you invested a few dollars. And for purely practical reasons, you'll be glad, too, since all that dirt wiped off on your fresh new mat is dirt that won't be tracked through your home.

Avoid doormats with "cute" sayings, and steer clear of those that proclaim things like "The Browns Welcome You." A simple "Welcome" is acceptable, but remember that you are setting a scene in which you want the buyer to imagine that the house is *his*, not yours. Advertising your name or initials is counterproductive, making it difficult for the buyer to fantasize that he, to paraphrase the old Hertz slogan, is in the owner's seat.

14. Open your home to the outside world.

As a buyer strolls up the front walk toward your home, he naturally wonders what he will discover behind your front door and whether he will like what he sees. As we've noted before, a buyer approaches a home with curiosity aroused; he wants to have positive feelings toward that house. If all the curtains are drawn and the front door is locked and bolted, your home will seem like a forbidding fortress. What are they trying to hide, your customer may well think to himself, without even realizing where the bad "vibes" are coming from.

If, on the other hand, the curtains are open, the windows sparkling clean, and the front door open in warm weather, your home will radiate a welcoming spirit and invite the buyer to enter. There's nothing nicer than the appearance of a center-hall home with both front and back doors open on a sunny day. The buyer can look through the screen doors and even catch a glimpse of the backyard awaiting him. But whatever he sees through your open front door—whether it be center hall, foyer, or a living room—make sure that the view is a pleasant and inviting one.

Of course, you don't have the open-door option in the winter, but you can make sure that all draperies are pulled back, shades are up, blinds are open. If you have side panels of glass by your front door, by all means remove curtains you may have hung there for privacy, and let your buyers have a peek while they're waiting for you to answer the door.

15. Capitalize on a spacious front porch.

If you are lucky enough to have an old-fashioned front porch, don't take it for granted. *Do* take advantage of the nostalgia it evokes. Many people associate a broad verandah with gentle and gracious living. Even if your family never uses the porch, your buyers may love the idea of having one.

At the very least, set out an old rocker or two, or find that ancient porch glider and place it there again. During the warm months, you can go all out and really capitalize on the front porch by setting out white wicker furniture if you're lucky enough to have some. Add a few bright pillows and some hanging plants between the columns. Since you're setting a scene, aid the buyer's imagination by leaving an open book on the porch swing or a needlework project on the seat of the rocking chair. Keep the floor uncluttered, of course, but a single doll carriage or hobby horse will suggest to the buyer that this is a great place for kids to play on rainy summer days.

Don't expect potential buyers to look at an empty porch and be able to visualize it in use. It's your responsibility to set the stage effectively and stimulate their imaginations. Start them playing the subconscious "If I Lived in This House" game right here on the porch, and you'll have them hooked.

It can't be emphasized enough: if a buyer can imagine himself living in your home, he's taken the first big step toward making you an offer.

Whether you have a graciously proportioned center-hall entry area or a small space just large enough for a coat rack and tiny table, this part of your home deserves your particular attention. A little tender loving care applied to this first glimpse potential buyers will have of your home's interior can pay off in big dividends. Remember the importance of first impressions: spruce up this entry area to be a gracious and attractive introduction to the rest of your home. If you turn off your buyer here, you may never get him back on the hook.

16. Create a dramatic focal point.

Study your entry hall with a critical eye and ask yourself what kind of statement it makes about the rest of your home. If that statement is "ho-hum," then you're missing a vital selling opportunity. This area of your home should greet buyers with something visually beautiful, something that says, "Welcome, your house-hunting days are over."

A spectacular arrangement of flowers appeals to a buyer's sense of smell as well as his sense of sight. If you have flowers on your property, by all means cut some for the entry hall—lilacs, roses, peonies, anything in season. If nothing is blooming, think about forcing some forsythia or flowering cherry, whatever is available. Be bold, and make this a dramatic statement. It should be noticed at once.

If you weren't born with a green thumb, you needn't order long-stemmed roses from your local florist every time your home is shown. Roadsides in your area may abound in seasonal wildflowers. Obviously, we're not talking about rare or endangered species, but rather the common ones like wild phlox or black-eyed susans that grow in profusion and make spectacular bouquets. And what's more, they're free for the taking. During winter

months, you might feature a dramatic Christmas cactus or poin-
settia.

If nothing live seems to be available, dried flowers can make a
striking focal point on a hall table any time of the year. Imagine
cattails, a branch of bright orange Chinese lanterns, an arching
spray of bittersweet, or wheat stalks in a glowing copper planter.
If you have lovely silk flowers, or want to invest in them, this is the
place to display them to best advantage—namely, *your* advantage
in selling your home.

An antique umbrella stand can be a delightful accent in a small
entry hall as well as being practical on rainy days. A bentwood
coat rack looks good with a few hats and a colorful scarf. Don't
weight it down with coats, which belong in the closet.

17. Add spaciousness with a mirror.

Virtually any entry hall, especially a very small one, will benefit
from a well-placed mirror. Not only will a mirror visually enlarge
the area, it will also add interesting dimensions by reflecting
another room or even the outdoors, depending on where it is
placed. The mirror will also double the impact of the dramatic
flower arrangement you've placed in front of it.

Of course, mirrors have their practical side, too. People do like
to check their appearance when they enter or leave the house.

The mirror here should be a rather special one. If you have an
attractive gilded picture frame, consider having a mirror put in it,
which can be done quite reasonably. Interesting frames are often
to be found at flea markets and antique shows for relatively little
money. Adding the mirror to such a "find" will certainly be much
cheaper than buying a pre-framed, brand-new mirror.

Finally, the whole effect will, of course, be spoiled if the mirror
doesn't gleam, so be sure to whip out the Windex every few days.

18. Improve the floor's appearance here, if nowhere else.

With the possible exception of the kitchen floor, your entry hall's
flooring will be observed more carefully than that in any other
room in your house. Buyers, having wiped their feet on your new
doormat, will instinctively look down at the floor upon entering
your home, and with the front door open and brilliant daylight
flooding the area, those scratches in the wood or worn spots in
the carpet will be unmercifully exposed.

These signs of neglect can easily create a first impression of shabbiness and plant seeds of doubt and wariness in a buyer's mind at the very beginning of the house tour. Since you want the prospective buyer going through your home with a positive attitude, don't give him anything to question this early in the game.

Take a long, hard look at your floors. If the wood floors are really badly scratched, you may have to rent a sander and refinish them. If the scratching is relatively minor, a good wax-and-polish job probably will do the trick. If you have carpeting here that is extremely worn, rip it up and replace it with an attractive area rug that you can take with you. (But be sure to tack it down so that you don't have an unexpected lawsuit on your hands!)

19. Clean out your coat closet.

This entry hall closet will be the first one to be inspected by potential buyers, so make it appear as roomy as possible by removing most of your family's coats. In spring or summer, there is no need to clutter up this closet with bulky parkas and ski jackets. Pare down your coat collection to the absolute minimum, and store the ones you're not using in the attic.

Bear in mind that this is a *coat* closet—and, in fact, used to be called a guest closet. Remove those skis, tennis racquets, bowling balls, fishing tackle, etc. Your crowded closet might do Fibber McGee proud, but it surely won't make your home sell faster.

Once you have visually enlarged your closet space by removing as much of its contents as possible, place a few extra hangers there in case buyers choose to shed their coats while viewing your house. But take a tip from Joan Crawford: No wire coat hangers, please—they do seem a bit cheap.

One finishing touch can improve the closet. Hang a bag of cedar chips or a pomander ball filled with potpourri to give a pleasant, fresh scent when the closet door is opened. Avoid moth balls here, however, since they smell rather harsh and may send some buyers into sneezing fits—not an auspicious way to begin the house tour.

20. Create the illusion of an entry hall if you have none.

When building costs began skyrocketing, some penny-wise, pound-foolish builders decided that entry halls were an unnecessary spatial luxury. If your home has this unfortunate drawback, do everything you can to counter the negative impression it will make upon most buyers.

You may have overlooked this drawback and learned to live with it, but most home buyers don't want to walk through a front door directly into the living room. An entry hall does serve some purpose, and not only as a reminder of a bygone time when living was gracious and less harried. The entry hall was a place to greet people, to take their coats, to drop your bundles, to leave a calling card, and, perhaps most important, a place to take some wear and tear off your living room. Except for calling cards, these functions still apply. Even though it means giving up some precious living room space, you should strongly consider rearranging your furniture to create the illusion of an entry hall.

To divide the space, you'll need a partial partition. This might be a narrow table, an open bookcase, a railing, an étagère. Don't invest in new furniture—make do with something you have. Try defining this space with the aid of an attractive small throw rug. Experiment with furniture arrangements until the area looks natural and uncluttered. If you opt for a narrow table to partition the space, add a floral arrangement to gain height without totally blocking the view into the living room. If you divide the space with a tall étagère, be sure you don't crowd the shelves with too much bric-a-brac. This should be an open partition that allows a buyer to look into the living room but *feel* that he is in a separate entry hall.

Another way to set this space apart from your living room is to make certain that the entry section has its own lighting, whether it be a small hanging fixture, two sconces on either side of a mirror, or an attractive ginger jar lamp on the "hall" table. Lighting can define spaces and help you to visually partition the two areas.

LIVING ROOM AND FAMILY ROOM

If the kitchen is the heart of any home, these rooms are surely close runners-up for that title. The living room may be rather more formal than the family room, but both are places around which family life is centered. Whether you use them for formal entertaining, for a cocktail party, for beer and pretzels on Saturday night, for playing with the kids, or just for watching television, they reflect deeply the kind of home you have made of your house, and the kind of home you are trying to sell. They deserve your very special attention.

21. Treat these rooms as if they were stage settings.

When prospective home buyers tour a house, there is one question they ask themselves upon entering each room: "Can I imagine myself *living* in this room?" Your job as an effective seller is to make each room project a positive response to that silent question. The best way to do this is to set the stage effectively to aid the buyer's imagination.

In general, you should aim for a happy medium between a too casual and a too formal look. Unfortunately, sellers usually err to one extreme or the other when they prepare these rooms for showing. Either the room has a sloppy, "lived-in" look, or it has been so depersonalized that the seller might as well hang a velvet rope across the doorway and charge admission.

Ask yourself what touches make a room look truly inviting, and then set the scene. Music is one thing that everyone can identify with, one element that makes any house a home. Consider leaning a guitar in the corner of your living room, or opening some sheet music on the piano with a light shining on it as though someone's practicing had just been interrupted. Games are another thing that indicate a good family life. How about a jigsaw puzzle in progress or a Trivial Pursuit board set up on a card table in the family room? Or leave a dictionary and a half-finished crossword puzzle on the coffee table. If knitting is your thing, a basket of needles and wool by the side of your wing chair will be quite effective in evoking positive responses from the buyer.

Think of these things as stage props. Use items that truly express your lifestyle, use them judiciously, and the buyer will surely respond by imagining himself living in your home. Once the buyer starts to see *your* house as *his* house, an offer is likely to follow.

22. Highlight your fireplace.

A fireplace is a "must" feature for almost every buyer, so if you have one, play it up for all it's worth. Don't take it for granted and expect the buyer to imagine the glow or a roaring fire; *light* one whenever the house is being shown. Obviously this doesn't apply when it's ninety degrees in the shade, but cool, rainy days all year 'round may warrant at least a small blaze to take the dampness out of the air. If you always have some kindling and logs set up, it's easy to light a fire when the agent calls to make a last-minute appointment. If you don't want to go to the bother of setting a fire every time the house is shown, at least keep a few Duraflame logs handy to light on short notice.

A glowing fire can't be ignored, but to complete the scene, why not pull up a cozy chair by the fireplace or set a couple of large, plump pillows on the floor in front of the hearth so that prospective buyers can imagine toasting themselves there on a cold winter's night.

When the wood-burning season is truly over, clean out the ashes and consider placing a lush fern or a dried flower arrangement on the hearth. If that doesn't appeal to you, what about a handsome fireplace fan? Or place something colorful on the mantel to attract the buyer's eye. Speaking of mantels, don't overdo it here by crowding the shelf with all kinds of bric-a-brac and family photographs. A few tasteful, well-selected items will be far more effective in highlighting your mantel. Be sure, too, that brass fixtures and utensils are polished to a fare-thee-well.

Remember that your fireplace is a very strong asset, and don't let it go unnoticed or unappreciated.

23. Improve traffic flow in these rooms.

Chances are that each time your home is shown, at least three people will be touring—a salesperson and a house-buying couple. Often, there will be even more people in this group—children, parents, friends, etc. It's therefore essential to consider your home's traffic flow, especially in your living room and family room where the most pieces of furniture, and often the bulkiest pieces, tend to accumulate.

If your furniture is big and amply scaled and crowded into a relatively small area, buyers will have to tour your home "Indian file," rather like a game of follow-the-leader. Needless to say, this can be extremely awkward for the prospective buyers, and will surely make your home seem smaller than it is. The obvious question that will pop into the buyer's mind is, "How in the world could I ever fit my furniture into this dollhouse?"

As mentioned earlier, you can make rooms seem visually larger by removing excess furniture. By all means do this if you can. But now is also the time when you should rearrange some pieces so that people can walk comfortably through your rooms without feeling cramped. It may be only a matter of pushing a couple of armchairs back a foot or so toward the walls; even that relatively small distance can make all the difference in creating an opening through which people can pass comfortably without suffering an attack of claustrophobia. Pay particular attention to entry and exit ways, and be sure that no large piece of furniture is intruding upon them.

Be sure, while you're at it, that all doors can open fully. If one opens halfway and bumps up against your massive Victorian commode, your customers may become a bit nervous—and nervous customers don't buy homes.

24. Draw attention to exposed beams or a cathedral ceiling.

Surprisingly, many buyers flit through houses without noticing the very things that the owners prize most, and this is not necessarily the buyer's fault. These unfocused buyers need you to direct their attention to your home's bestselling features. One may be an attractive ceiling. Getting the buyer to look up can take a bit of doing.

If your home has handsome exposed beams, make sure that buyers raise their heads and notice them. Draw eyes upwards by hanging something from the beams. Depending on your decor, you might take a cue from our Colonial forebears and hang baskets, copper or cast-iron pots, herbs, or dried flowers. If this is too traditional for your contemporary home, consider hanging a dramatic mobile, a chandelier, or simply houseplants. Spider plants, with their long, trailing plantlets might look especially good in this context.

You can also accomplish the same goal with well-directed lighting. A couple of small spotlights aimed toward the ceiling will sharply define those exposed beams and draw the buyer's eye directly to them. You should not hesitate to leave such lights on during the daylight hours when most of your homeshowing will take place. It will be well worth the pennies spent on electricity.

A soaring cathedral ceiling is a spectacular asset, which you should definitely capitalize on. Use the suggestions offered for highlighting beams, but keep scale in mind. Since the cathedral ceiling is so much higher, you can afford to be bolder with your lighting as well as with anything you may choose to hang from the apex. Be as inventive and imaginative as you can in order to make your ceiling a real selling plus.

25. Don't let a television set dominate the room.

Television may have revolutionized the entertainment habits of the world, but let's face it: most television sets are ugly! Unless you're willing and able to spend thousands of dollars for state-of-the-art electronics, you're probably living with a big wooden box with a big glassy screen stuck in the middle of it. Portables are easy enough to tuck out of sight, but if you have a console, you may have a problem when showing your house.

What to do? It isn't necessary to get rid of the TV, but you should think of downplaying it as much as possible. If your cabinet has doors on it, by all means close them to hide the screen. If the top of the set is chock-a-block with family photographs, World's Fair souvenirs, and the conch shell you found at the beach last summer, sweep them away to some less conspicuous spot. One discreet vase or plant or piece of sculpture here might be attractive, but too much bric-a-brac only draws unwanted attention to the "box."

If your television is usually in the middle of the room for better viewing, roll it back to a corner and find a storage system for all the wires, paddles, game cartridges, etc. Maybe your kids would disagree, but under the circumstances, you don't want your room looking like a video arcade. And remember that your potential buyer is much more interested in the size of your room than the size of your television screen or the extent of your Atari game collection.

DINING ROOM OR DINING AREA

"So this is the dining room," proclaims a bewildered husband in a popular commercial for frozen dinners. Could this indicate a trend? Are Americans rediscovering their dining rooms after years of informal meals at the kitchen table or on TV snack trays? There seems to be renewed interest in dining as an art these days. So spruce up your dining room—it's back in fashion!

26. Set the scene by setting the table.

You can stimulate a buyer's imagination by setting your dining table with pretty china and silver. This easy task can transform an ordinary dining room into a warm and welcoming one that appeals on an emotional level to a buyer's fantasies, conjuring up images of gracious entertaining and friendly family gatherings.

Why not employ this subtle selling edge when showing your home? It takes only a few minutes to set an attractive table, and the results are well worth the extra effort. Notice the photographs of dining rooms in any home decorating magazine. The tables are always set appealingly. Why? Because this simple trick personalizes a dining room and makes it possible for you, the viewer, to imagine yourself living in this setting.

If your home is being shown in the morning, the table should be cheerful and informal, as if set for a casual luncheon. Picture brightly colored placemats, plaid napkins, chunky stoneware, and a pitcher filled with daisies as a centerpiece. Buyers will respond by wanting to pull up a chair and make themselves at home.

When you show your home in the afternoon, your table might be set more formally, as if ready for a family dinner. Whatever the occasion, always avoid going overboard. A table set for twelve with elegant Waterford crystal and your finest Lenox china is too fancy in all but the most formal of homes. Any stage setting that you create should reflect the character of your entire home if it is to be effective.

27. Make a large dining room do double duty.

If your home has a particularly large dining room, you are very lucky, so by all means take advantage of those generous proportions and give the room extra sales appeal by selecting a corner where you can create a "room-within-a-room." Although your dining room may be the perfect size for your family of ten, some buyers will view a large dining room as wasted space, especially if the other rooms in your home are relatively smaller.

Consider moving that secretary desk out of your overcrowded living room and into a corner of your dining room to create the illusion of a private "den." Simply add a small lamp and an open box of stationery to complete the picture, so that buyers can imagine enjoying this special area of your home. If a buyer's response is, "What a lovely place to sit and pay my bills," your dining room has doubled its sales appeal.

How about that old spinet piano in the basement, which hasn't been touched since your daughter gave up music lessons in favor of karate? Why not move it into your dining room to create an instant music corner? Dust off the ivories, set out some sheet music, and let buyers imagine having their own afternoon musicales.

A dining room can also perform double duty as a family "library." All you need to do is move a comfortable chair into a cozy corner, add a reading lamp and a magazine rack or small bookcase, and you have the perfect stage setting for buyers to picture themselves curled up with the latest bestseller on a rainy afternoon. It may be difficult at first to imagine your dining room serving another function, but once you've made the adjustment, you'll wonder why you never thought of it before. And you'll impress a lot of potential home buyers.

28. Visually enlarge a small dining area.

A skimpy dining area is a more common problem and a definite drawback, so take some corrective measures before agents and customers try squeezing their way between your dining table and massive breakfront. Keeping in mind the fact that several people will be touring your dining area at the same time, improve the traffic flow as best you can after considering these tips:

—If your dining table has removable leaves, take one or two out when buyers are viewing your home. A smaller table will make the room look larger and make it much easier for people to walk through the area comfortably.

—Consider placing your dining table against a wall rather than positioning it in the center of the room. This will work best with a drop-leaf table.

—Remove any extra "company" side chairs. If your dining area is very small, the only chairs you need to have in the room are those at the table that you use every day. Company chairs that you use only for entertaining should be stored elsewhere while your house is being shown.

—If you inherited a matched dining set of several humongous pieces, chances are they are crowding your dining area and making the room seem even smaller than it is. Consider putting that looming china cabinet in storage until your house is sold.

After improving your dining area's traffic flow, see if there are other ways to enlarge the space visually. Since clutter can make a room seem smaller, clear the top surfaces of any sideboards or serving counters. One simple silver or cut-glass bowl filled with fruit is plenty of decoration in a small area. Aim for a clean and tidy look. If you have a glassfront china cabinet, make sure the shelves are not crammed with items. Store extra china and glasses to obtain that all-important uncluttered look.

Since bright, sunny rooms always appear larger, be sure you let as much light as possible into your small dining area. Curtains should not be heavy, and windows (sparkling clean, of course) should not be blocked by too many plants. Try hanging a mirror on the wall opposite the window. It will reflect an outdoor scene, making the room look larger and more open.

Your Home's

KITCHEN

In the good old pioneering days of our country, family life centered around the kitchen. Today, hundreds of years later, the kitchen continues to be the heart of the home. It is the room where family and friends just naturally seem to congregate.

A pleasant, working kitchen is near the top of most buyers' list of priorities. In fact, real estate agents used to joke among themselves, "Sell the wife on the kitchen and the husband will buy the house." Even in these less chauvinistic times, a terrific kitchen can still sell a house, so any time you spend improving yours is time well spent.

29. Use props to set a cheerful scene.

Cold, antiseptic kitchens simply don't appeal to most buyers. Even if their culinary expertise is limited to heating frozen dinners in a microwave oven, buyers want a kitchen to *look* like a kitchen. The most modern, utilitarian kitchen should still have those homey touches that make the room inviting, so set the scene with a few carefully selected props:

—An open cookbook
—A copper colander filled with blueberries
—A basket of eggs
—A bunch of carrots on a wooden cutting board
—A hanging wire basket filled with onions
—A ceramic mixing bowl and wire whisk

Some people seem to think that all traces of food should be tucked out of sight when the kitchen is shown, but nothing could be further from the truth. Food is what kitchens are all about, what draws people to them, and often what evokes fond memories of childhood after-school snacks and midnight binges. So don't hesitate to use food as a prop to help sell your house. A

kitchen is for cooking and eating, and should reflect those pur-
poses in a charming, attractive manner.

30. Make it smell like Grandma's kitchen.

To quote another popular commercial, "Nothing says lovin' like
something from the oven." Let's face it, all of us have early memories of kitchen aromas that can still make us wax nostalgic—
homemade bread, gingerbread cookies, apple pie, etc. Which-
ever is your favorite, all of these aromas are associated with
happiness and a sense of well-being. As an effective seller, you
should fill your kitchen with a richly evocative scent, one that
will appeal to the nostalgic yearnings of buyers.

Not that you must bake fresh bread every time your home is
shown—not even James Beard would go that far. If you opt for
baking bread, the simplest way to fill your kitchen with this
aroma is to keep commercial frozen bread dough in your refrig-
erator, the kind you buy in the freezer section of your supermar-
ket, ready to be popped into your oven on a moment's notice.

If baking bread seems too clichéd a nostalgic prop, a more
original kitchen aroma can be created on top of your stove.
Specially blended packages of dried herbs and spices, with
names like Skiers' Brew or Christmas Brew, are often available in
stores around holiday time. When added to simmering water,
they release scents with wonderful nostalgic appeal. If you can't
locate these mixtures, it's very easy to invent your own. Simply
decide which aroma you want to feature (be it cinnamon, ginger,
nutmeg, what have you), and toss a handful of herbs and spices
into a pot of simmering water. Your brew need only be con-
cocted once; just refrigerate it between showings and warm it up
at the last minute.

Here's a mix guaranteed to have buyers longing to whip up a
batch of cookies in *your* kitchen:

GRANNY'S AROMATIC SECRET

1 whole nutmeg
5 cinnamon sticks
1 tablespoon whole allspice
1 tablespoon whole cloves

Halve the nutmeg and add all ingredients to 3 cups water
in a saucepan. Bring to a boil, then lower to simmer.

In the heat of summer, when the scents of baking bread and

simmering cinnamon may seem a bit too heavy, a bowl of lemons on the counter will provide a fresh and pleasant aroma. Or, simplest of all, just brew a pot of fresh coffee before buyers arrive. It hearty scent appeals to almost everyone, even non-coffee drinkers.

Although you may love the smell of onions and garlic cooking in oil, many people do not. Stick with the "safe" aromas, and be sure to remove strong cooking odors from your kitchen with the aid of a stove exhaust, an air filter, or simply an open window. Setting the right olfactory scene for your customers is an important part of the home-selling process.

31. Expand your counter space.

Few kitchens have adequate counter space, particularly for those aspiring four-star chefs whose cooking rivals Julia Child's. If your kitchen is short on counter space, the problem will be less obvious if you clear your counters of all small appliances. When your home is being shown, store your coffee grinder, can opener, kitchen scale, toaster, food processor, or whatever, in a cabinet, so that your counters will be clear and seem more spacious. If you have a dish-draining rack on the counter next to your sink, stash that away under the sink while buyers tour your home. Check the counter top around your sink, and remove any bottles of dish detergent or cans of cleanser that may be cluttering the area.

If you have taken all these steps and your counter space still seems meager, consider investing in an inexpensive hinged table top, which can be installed against a wall to serve as an extra working surface. Be sure to have this supplementary "counter" extended when buyers tour your kitchen so that they will notice it. If your kitchen is large but designed with inadequate counter space, look into buying a movable cart with butcher-block top that can serve as extra working space. Since this is not a permanent fixture, you'll be entitled to take it with you, or sell it to the new owners.

32. Create more storage space.

No matter how much storage space you have in your kitchen, if your cabinets, drawers, and closets are jammed full, buyers will get the impression that your storage space is inadequate. Therefore, your first step must be to weed out all these storage areas, getting rid of what you don't ever use, storing seldom-used items elsewhere, and reorganizing shelves with oft-used items. Neat, organized shelves and drawers fool the eye by looking larger than they do when packed with foodstuffs and kitchen paraphernalia.

There are several inexpensive storage solutions on the market today. One is a hanging pot rack designed to hang over a stove or in a corner. These racks can hold up to ten pots and pans, thus freeing your cabinet space. An excellent solution to crowded drawers is a plastic grid system that hangs flat against your wall with hooks to hold spatulas, mixing and measuring spoons, whisks, etc. Another handy space-expanding item is a lazy susan for spices, small packages, glasses, or whatever.

Don't hesitate to invest in these storage options if they will make your kitchen appear larger and better organized. Although you may have learned to live with your kitchen's drawbacks over the years, don't expect a potential buyer to fall in love with a poorly organized kitchen.

33. Accent kitchen windows.

Large, cheerful kitchen windows are a real plus and should be highlighted as a special feature of your home. A sunny window is the perfect place to grow a miniature herb garden. Parsley and chives couldn't be easier to grow, and they add a charming culinary touch to your decor as well as drawing the buyer's eye toward your pleasant kitchen windows.

If you'd rather not try to keep plants alive, hang a stained glass mobile or some wind chimes in front of your sunny kitchen window, or line the sill with pretty glass bottles that will reflect the light.

If you hang a bird feeder outside your window, nature will seem to become a part of the room, and the constant avian activity will lend a special delight to your kitchen. Fill the feeder with sunflower and thistle seeds in the winter and attract troops of friendly chickadees and finches. In the spring and early summer, set out bits of string and colorful yarns, which birds will carry off for nest building. Place a pair of binoculars and a field guide on the window sill, and you'll be surprised to find how many potential buyers will share your interest, taking delight in the fact that your home is already an established bird sanctuary.

34. Make a small kitchen appear larger.

If your home was built during the period when kitchens were designed to be small and functional, do everything you can to visually enlarge your kitchen space.

Consider repainting the kitchen all white to give it a fresh, clean, uncluttered look. Unify your color scheme by painting the walls, ceiling, and cabinets the same color. The all-white decor will seem to make the walls and ceiling recede, fooling the eye into seeing a larger room. Use kitchen props sparingly within this small space—a couple of colorful accents will probably be enough. Your curtains should be light in weight and color to blend right into your walls. Or consider removing them completely so that you let in a maximum amount of sunlight. As always, a strategically placed mirror, probably across from the window, will help to expand your space.

After you have done everything possible to make your kitchen appear larger, sit back and stop worrying. There are buyers who appreciate an economical kitchen layout—a professional couple with little interest in cooking, or an older couple who will love the step-saving convenience of a smaller kitchen. And remember above all, *never* apologize for any of your home's shortcomings!

35. Highlight an eat-in area of your kitchen.

If you've got it, flaunt it! Nothing could be truer in today's world of home-selling when it comes to a large, eat-in kitchen. Today's buyers seem to love the idea of oversized kitchens with plenty of space for casual, pre-dinner visiting.

At the very top of almost any buyer's list of desirable kitchen features is a generously scaled "breakfast room" set off from the work area. If your home has this pleasant asset, accentuate it by setting the table for an informal meal with bright placemats and a generous bowl of fruit as a centerpiece. These colorful props will immediately draw your customer's eye to this very special area of your kitchen. To complete the picture, try engaging the buyer's imagination with a crossword puzzle book, newspaper, or magazine beside the place setting. Suggest in any way you can that this is a warm and homey spot to linger over a second cup of coffee.

Almost all but the tiniest efficiency kitchens can be arranged to accommodate an eat-in area, even if this is nothing more than two stools pulled up to a counter. If you can make room for this feature in your kitchen, by all means do so. Purchase two inexpensive, unfinished stools, paint them a vibrant color that contrasts with your kitchen's basic decor, and position them in front of a counter on which you've set a couple of cheerful placemats. You'll find that young parents like the idea of being able to feed their youngsters in the kitchen, and that many buyers enjoy having a spot in the kitchen where they can perch and grab a sandwich, talk on the phone, or make up a grocery list.

LAUNDRY ROOM

A separate laundry room, even if it's not much larger than a walk-in closet, is a true asset and one that is appreciated by all buyers. Don't hide this treasure behind closed doors when your house is being shown. Spruce up the room and leave the door proudly open for inspection.

36. Make it cheerful and appealing.

Washing, drying, and ironing the family's clothing may be rather dreary chores, but there's no reason why your home's laundry room has to reflect a negative attitude. If you've always thought of your laundry room as being purely functional and, let's face it, boring, stop right now and rethink these notions before you show your home. Since each and every room should contribute to selling your home, don't neglect the lowly laundry room. A little inexpensive revamping can make it a strong selling feature.

Does your laundry room need a fresh coat of paint? Chances are it does, if you're like most homeowners who never take the time to add some sparkle to this area of the house. One can of paint can do wonders for this room. Just be sure to choose a bright, light, cheerful color like sunshine yellow or robin's egg blue. If the room has a window, accentuate this plus by purchasing a pair of inexpensive checked cotton curtains to coordinate with the wall color.

Be sure the room is well organized before you start showing your home. No matter how appealing you have made this area, piles of dirty clothes can be a real turn-off to the buyer's eye—and his nose! Dirty clothes should be in the washer or in closed hampers, and freshly laundered clothing should be on hangers or folded in neat piles. Be sure, too, that the room smells fresh and is bright enough to give a cheerful appearance. Increase the wattage of light bulbs if necessary.

37. Set it up to do double duty.

Victorian architects were particularly clever at designing delightful hideaways where each family member could stake a claim to one special corner of the home that was his or hers alone. Unfortunately, in today's homes, space is at a premium, making it difficult for people to carve a personal niche for their private pursuits or daydreams.

If your laundry room is large and there's room in the corner for a table and chair, convert this dead space into a positive selling feature. Could it be made into a pleasant sewing area? Set up that old Singer in the corner, open it up, plug it in, and place a bright-colored piece of fabric under the presser foot. Instant sewing room! Is there room for a card table? Move your son's or daughter's latest model airplane kit into this corner, suspend a completed plane or two from the ceiling, and you've suddenly created a hobby room! Or perhaps this room could double as a potting shed. All you need is a table or counter set up with some clay pots, bags of potting soil, and a few low-light plants.

As you can see, the possibilities are endless. It's up to you to make use of any extra space your home offers, then set up a scene to stimulate a buyer's imagination. Too many sellers expect buyers to be able to visualize a room's potential uses. Don't fall into that lazy trap. Set the stage so that a buyer's *instant* reaction is, "I've always wanted a sewing-room hide-away far from the din of the TV. What a nice feature!"

Your Home's
STAIRWAYS

Stairways should provide an attractive transition from one level of your home to another. Make sure your stairways are well lit and cheerfully decorated, so that a buyer's sense of anticipation is heightened as he climbs or descends the steps to explore another floor in your home. Needless to say, dark and boring stairways will not make your house sell faster, so check them out and take corrective measures to add some sales appeal to these often neglected areas of the house.

38. Make them safe.

The last thing you need when you're trying to sell your home is a lawsuit instigated by a disgruntled buyer who has tumbled down your stairs. Make a safety check of each of your home's stairways. And don't neglect your basement steps; these are often the steepest, darkest, and thus most dangerous in your home.

- —Be sure the lighting in any staircase is *more* than adequate. Increase the wattage of bulbs, or add supplementary light fixtures if necessary. Do your checking on a gloomy, overcast day.
- —Stairs *must* be clutter-free. If your family is in the habit of leaving clothes and toys on bottom steps, crack the whip and lay down the law while your house is on the market. Litter on steps is not only hazardous, it can make your stairway look narrower and less attractive.
- —Check your stair railing to be sure that it's tight and secure. A wobbly rail is dangerous and reflects poorly on your home's upkeep.
- —Stair runners or carpeting must be tacked securely in place. Get down on your hands and knees for a close inspection of every step to verify that the carpet is well attached.

39. Add visual interest to the stairwell.

Take a minute to study the primary staircase in your home, and consider whether a carefully chosen accent might improve the area's visual appeal. If you're fortunate enough to have a wide, gracious staircase, emphasize this feature by hanging a few pictures along the wall. Draw attention to a handsome lighting fixture by polishing the brass and dusting each small light bulb or crystal prism. (Of course you'll turn on this light while viewers inspect your home.) Any stair landing should also have an attractive focal point, be it a fern on a plantstand, a dramatic poster, a chiming clock, or a special chair on a large stair landing. If the stairwell is deep, a mobile can add dramatic interest. Take stock of *your* staircase, and add the accent that will best punch up its appeal. As usual, borrow from other rooms of your house.

But what if your staircase is narrow? Fool the eye by minimizing clutter. Remember that a wall crammed with a hodgepodge of pictures will make a narrow staircase look even narrower. Decorative accents in small areas should be quiet and understated rather than bold and assertive. Wallpaper can have the same narrowing effect, so perhaps you should consider covering those cabbage roses with a couple of coats of light-colored paint.

If you have young children, remember that dirty little finger smudges do not qualify as "visual interest." Clean up all signs of youngsters' palm prints with cleanser or a fresh coat of paint.

40. Improve the appearance of stair treads.

Shabby stair treads have no place in a well-maintained home. If your stair's carpeting is soiled and worn, first try to save it with a good stiff cleaning. However, if the nap is almost nonexistent and the backing is beginning to show, tear up the carpeting and see what you can do to improve the appearance of the bare wood steps.

Chances are that if your stairs have always been carpeted, the wood underneath may need only a light waxing to bring out its natural beauty, or at most a simple sanding and coat of wood stain to make the steps look brand new again.

If yours is an older home, you may find that the stairs were painted years ago. In that case, don't even think about refinishing the stairs in what will soon be someone else's house: the simplest solution is another coat of paint to freshen up their appearance. If the risers are painted white or a light color, check for scuff marks and touch up with a new coat of paint.

Badly scratched and worn stair treads and risers call for more drastic measures. It will pay to invest in a new stair runner to cover the shabby wood. Since most runners are not as wide as the total width of your stairs, be sure to touch up the portion of wood that will be showing at either side of the new runner.

Imagine for a moment that you're in the "bed-and-breakfast" business. How would you change your home's bedrooms to appeal to a paying lodger? Naturally you'd make up the beds with your prettiest sheets and comforters. Maybe you'd add a vase of flowers on the dressing table or a cozy armchair in the corner.

A smart seller applies the same principles to making his home more salable. Every bedroom in your home should invite prospective buyers to settle right in and spend the night. Even children's rooms should be irresistible. So take the time to survey your bedrooms with an innkeeper's savvy eye and put them to work for you.

41. Create a master bedroom "suite" effect.

Large master bedrooms are particularly popular among today's home buyers, and are therefore a very strong selling feature. Concentrate on making your largest bedroom look even larger by applying some of the suggestions offered earlier in this book: i.e., paint the room a light color; remove one of the bureaus if the room is crowded; minimize clutter to maximize spaciousness. Since any room will look larger if decorated in tones of one color, try to coordinate your bedspread with the wall and carpet colors. Avoid as much as possible "busy" patterns in small rooms, as well as distracting riots of color. Instead, aim for a restful, subdued "look."

If at all possible, create a "living room" within a bedroom by adding a small writing desk in the corner where buyers can imagine themselves catching up on correspondence after the kids have gone to school. Or add a reading chair, a lamp, and, as a prop, an Agatha Christie on the chair, so that buyers can picture themselves engrossed in a good read on a cloudy day. A couple of café chairs and a small table set with a coffee pot and demitasse cups might suggest a romantic tête-à-tête with one's spouse.

A private bathroom off the master bedroom is a real sales plus. Ideally this bath should be decorated to coordinate with the color scheme of your bedroom, thus becoming a part of the total "suite" effect. Be sure to leave this bathroom door partially ajar when buyers view your home. Believe it or not, some prospective buyers are shy about opening closed doors, and so they may miss this bestselling feature if they mistake the closed door for a closet. Don't count on real estate salespeople to point out *all* your home's special features to reticent buyers; it's up to you to make rooms sell themselves.

42. Tackle your closets.

Does your home have adequate closet space? It's a rare home owner who can truthfully answer yes to this question. Since virtually all buyers are looking for a home with plenty of closet space, try to make what you have appear generous and well planned. Consider these common-sense guidelines:

—Clear out all but your current seasonal wardrobe so that your closet doesn't look crammed with clothes. Donate outgrown or outmoded clothing to your favorite charity, or try selling it at your yard sale. Clothing for other seasons should be stored elsewhere—perhaps in garment bags in the basement or attic—creating the impression that there is closet space for still more clothes. A few empty hangers will further this illusion.

—Since a clear floor will make a closet seem more spacious, invest in inexpensive shoe bags or racks, which will organize your collection and keep it off the floor.

—Closet shelves should look well organized. If your shelves contain a jumble of sweaters, socks, and hats, buy a few attractive storage boxes and organize your shelves before your closet becomes a neatnik's nightmare.

—When prospective buyers open your closet door, they should be greeted with a whiff of fresh-smelling air. As recommended earlier for the coat closet, try hanging a bag of cedar chips or pomander balls filled with potpourri in the back of your bedroom closet. Track down offensive odors and eliminate the sources (dirty sneakers and moth balls are two common offenders).

—Be sure that every closet in your home has a light so that buyers can easily inspect the interiors—don't count on a sunny day. Be sure your light bulbs haven't burned out or, if your closets don't have lights, pick up a couple of easily installed closet lights from your local hardware store. Little touches like this contribute mightily to creating the impression of a well-maintained home.

43. Invest in underbed storage boxes.

Living in a home that is on the market is a bit like living in a goldfish bowl, difficult for even the neatest of families. Invariably your real estate agent will call at the worst possible time to announce that he or she has the "perfect buyer" who wants to see your home in *ten minutes*. You then tear through your home like a whirling dervish trying to make the rooms look halfway presentable, and what do you find? Your teenage daughter has tried on every outfit she owns before leaving for school, and has left her bed piled high with the rejects. Or your six-year-old has dragged out every toy in his vast collection, leaving his bedroom resembling Santa's workshop on the day before Christmas.

Inexpensive underbed storage boxes are a godsend for the harried homeseller. In two shakes of a lamb's tail, you can sweep everything into these boxes, then slide them under the beds—one place where buyers never think to look. When you're pressed for time, these handy underbed catchalls can make your bedrooms look beautifully uncluttered.

Use underbed storage to alleviate crowded closets and attics. If your home is short on storage space (and whose isn't?), there's no sense in advertising this fact to prospective buyers. Use that hidden space under your beds to make your home appear neat and more spacious.

44. Depersonalize teenagers' rooms.

This notion may sound a bit controversial, and perhaps it is, but if you actively involve your children in the house-selling process from the very beginning, you should find them amenable to changes that will make their rooms—and hence your house—

more salable. This is not a matter of censorship, only a temporary measure that will ultimately be to everyone's benefit. So take the time to explain your house-selling goals to your children. Encourage them to participate in preparing your home for showing; and discuss with them some of the sales tips mentioned in this book, particularly the principle of appealing to the widest possible market.

Chances are that the only negative feature of your teen's room is sloppiness, and if that is the case, you're one up on the parents whose teen has decorated liberally with black paint and flashing strobe lights. If, for example, your daughter's room falls into the outlandishly bizarre category of decor, enlist her cooperation in "neutralizing" the appearance of her room.

Try to avoid a widening of the generation gap by explaining calmly that there are many buyers with a poor sense of imagination, who are not able to visualize a teenager's room as a dainty nursery or a quiet, understated guest room. Be clear and logical about the fact that your daughter's room will appeal to *more* buyers if it is decorated more conservatively, and assure her that individuality may once again run rampant when you move into your new home. If you treat house-selling as a family project, your teens will be more willing to join in and cooperate, even if it means storing their Boy George and *Night of the Living Dead* posters until your home is sold.

BATHROOMS

It's all too easy to take a bathroom for granted, to think of it as merely a functional closet to be cleaned regularly and then forgotten. Wise sellers, however, will take special pains with preparing their bathroom(s) for scrutiny by strangers. The bathroom is a room, after all, and a very personal one. Potential buyers will inspect yours with eagle eyes.

Any buyer will be put off by even a slightly grungy bathroom, so be sure yours is absolutely immaculate. Don't forget the medicine cabinet: dispose of those three-year-old prescriptions, and polish the shelves. The same goes for the storage cabinet under the sink. If cleanliness is next to godliness, your bathroom should be a shrine.

45. Create a look.

Since a bathroom is indeed a room, it not only needs to be cleaned, it needs to be decorated like any other room of the house. This doesn't mean that you have to retile the walls and lay in new vinyl at great expense. With a little imagination, it's easy and relatively cheap to personalize a bathroom. And that's the key word: personalize. Give your bathroom a pleasing, individual look, which can be done in any number of ways. Here are just a few of them:

- —Decorate with plants. Consider hanging a lush, green Boston fern by the window. Ferns thrive on the moisture they will find in abundance in the bathroom. If you have window shelves, fill them with small flowering plants such as African violets.
- —Display the shells you collected at the beach last summer in an attractive glass bowl or jar.
- —Don't forget that bathrooms, like any rooms, look more

homey and welcoming with pictures on the wall. Consider hanging a small grouping of delicate botanical prints.

—Do you have an old wooden coat rack? Paint it to coordinate with your bathroom color scheme, and hang fresh towels from it.

—If your bathroom is large and rather uninteresting, a brightly patterned beach towel pulled taut over artist's wooden canvas-stretcher bars gives a dramatic poster-look to that large bare wall.

—Add a magazine rack in the corner.

If your bathroom is very small, use restraint in adding accessories; a busy look will make the room appear even smaller.

46. Consider color.

All people have color likes and dislikes, but unfortunately in the world of home decorating, colors come and go, like sunspots and locusts, in cycles. Yesterday's "in" color may well be today's eyesore. While you may still adore your bathroom's flamingo sink, toilet, tub, and tiles, some buyers may have a strong aversion to wall-to-wall pink. This doesn't mean that you have to start tearing out fixtures and tiles, but you should remember that it's to your advantage to make your home appeal to as wide a range of buyers as possible. What to do? Play down that all-pink look with contrasting dove-gray towels and matching bathroom rug.

If, on the other hand, your bathroom walls and fixtures are white or neutral, add a few cheerful accents of color. Experiment with mixing towels in the popular new ice-cream sherbet shades or a spectrum of rainbow hues. Don't hesitate to buy a few new towels and a rug; you'll be taking them with you to your new home.

47. Invest in a new shower curtain.

You'd be surprised how many sellers overlook their tired, limp, often musty-smelling shower curtains, but *buyers notice*. Be sure your shower curtain looks fresh and coordinates with your revamped bathroom. Check your shower liner, too, and replace one with any signs of mildew. While you're at it, check your bathmat and replace it if necessary.

48. Improve your floor covering.

Notice the word is "improve," not "replace." There are some low-cost and convenient ways to make your floor look more inviting. Old worn vinyl or matted bathroom carpeting gives the room a seedy look and will detract from the fresh new accents you've added. Scrub and wax the old floor until it gives out as much shine as possible, and then cover the largest area you can with a generously sized scatter rug. If you spring for a complete coverup with bathroom carpeting—and this can be quite inexpensive for a small room—remember that buyers may expect you to leave it. Area rugs you can always take.

49. Put out fresh towels and soap.

Prospective buyers are very special guests in your home. Give them the VIP treatment with fresh-smelling towels and new soap in an attractive dish. Don't just put out another bar of Dial by the sink. Splurge on a box of fancy sculptured or perfumed guest soaps, and always provide fresh ones for each new set of customers. Be prepared by keeping those special soaps and guest towels tucked away in the linen closet, ready to be whipped out before each showing.

50. Go easy on air sprays and room deodorizers.

Some of these products are so overwhelming they can make you feel nauseous. Many of them contain inhalents to which allergic people are highly sensitive. Don't risk offending such a buyer with a strong dose of "Strawberry Surprise" or "Piney Paradise." A gentle hint of something in the air is fine, but keep it subtle. A pretty glass dish of potpourri should be sufficient. (You can buy "essential oils" in the same fragrance to refresh that potpourri.)

Whether it's an enormous, high-ceilinged room or a crawl space for storage under the eaves, your attic area will be examined closely by prospective buyers, and therefore should not detract from the well-kept appearance of the rest of your house. If your attic is reached by a steep flight of stairs, be sure they're clutter-free and well lit; if your attic crawl space is reached by a folding set of stairs that you pull down from the ceiling, be sure the mechanism is well oiled and there is adequate lighting.

51. Erase that creepy, haunted-house feeling.

Picture this scenario: You open the door leading to the attic and it creaks on its hinges; you reach for the light cord and the bulb is burned out; you begin climbing the stairs, only to be enveloped in a sticky spider web. This scene belongs in a grade B horror movie, not in your home when buyers are inspecting your attic.

Because many of them don't have windows, attics are creepy enough when clean, so for heaven's sake, spruce up your attic space, hide the mousetraps, and install bright lights. You don't want prospective buyers thinking they've wandered onto the set of *The Amityville Horror*.

If your attic does have windows, be sure to clean off the grime and let in as much light as possible. Take a broom and attack the cobwebs and old wasps' nests between the rafters, then sweep up any trace of, you should pardon the expression, rodent droppings.

52. Rearrange your storage.

Piles of boxes, stacks of yellowing newspapers, trunks overflowing with old clothes, fifty years' accumulation of *National Geographic*—these things constitute a pyromaniac's dream! Understand that most home owners (and home buyers) are terrified of fires, and then do everything you can to prevent your attic from looking like prospective tinder. The only buyers who might be attracted to such a cluttered attic are antique lovers who dream of finding a long-lost Rembrandt etching among your grand-mothers's collectables.

Clean out your attic and get rid of anything that you don't plan to take with you to your new home. Remaining stored materials should be neatly contained in boxes and trunks and positioned against the walls of your attic space, not out in the center of the room where people may easily trip. Since buyers adore the idea of having *tons* of storage space, your attic will appeal to them more if it seems to have been designed for pack rats.

53. Make the most of your attic's expansion potential.

If your home has a large, cheerful, windowed attic, you're sitting on a potential gold mine. Although your family may never have needed this area as extra living space, you can bet that many prospective buyers will be thrilled to have an extra bedroom, an old-fashioned playroom, or a hobby room for an elaborate electric train set-up.

There's no need to totally renovate your attic (chances are you would never recoup that financial investment anyway). Just put out a few props that will suggest to a buyer that your attic space has terrific potential as, for example, an extra bedroom. If you have an old mattress and boxspring, set them up and throw a bedspread over them; hang some curtains in the window and move an old table or bureau (how about the good one you've removed from your master bedroom?) to create a makeshift bed-room tableau.

Your attic might also suggest a delightful playroom if you dust off your kids' old puppet stage, set out some crates as theater seats, and prop up a blackboard as a theater marquee. Watch buyers' eyes light up when your little scene suggests a happy way to keep their children occupied on a winter afternoon.

"But why go to all that trouble?" you may ask. It is true that most buyers will walk into a big attic and think, "What a large room—maybe we could use it for something other than storage." What you are doing by setting up a scene with a few carefully selected props is stimulating the buyer's imagination so that he will see the room in a new and more attractive light.

Your Home's
BASEMENT

If your home has a full basement, chances are that the "machinery" of your home—furnace, water heater, electrical circuit breakers, etc.—is located there. Since educated buyers will inspect this area of your home with a fine-tooth comb, never stint here on necessary cleanup and repair. Spend a Saturday morning cleaning out your basement. Get rid of broken tools, rusted lawn furniture, and other assorted debris that has accumulated over the years. Give your basement a thorough sweeping, and organize your storage areas to present a tidy appearance. As a final touch, take a damp cloth and wipe off any dust or grime from the surface of your water heater and furnace—they'll look newer!

54. Make it as pleasant as possible.

No matter how lovely your home is, if it's sitting atop a dark, damp, musty-smelling basement, you're going to have trouble selling. One whiff of mildew and a prospective buyer may begin conjuring up scenes of wading through your flooded basement in rubber hip boots. If you've had water trouble in your basement and have corrected the problem with the installation of a sump pump, be sure to erase all signs of the old dampness. Clean up mildew stains, throw out any upholstered furniture that retains that musty smell, and check the basement walls for high water marks. You certainly don't want to advertise the fact that you had three feet of water in your basement before you purchased a sump pump. If necessary, give your basement walls a fresh coat of paint.

Many basements are creepy simply because they're too dark. If your basement has casement windows, they should be washed like every other window in the house, not left dusty on the inside and mud-splattered on the outside. Increase the wattage of your existing light bulbs, and if the room still has gloomy corners, install a few more lights.

Needless to say, mousetraps should be out of sight as well as
your pet's litter box. Basements don't have to be a turn-off.

55. Set it up as a gameroom or teen room.

A generously sized basement may provide just that extra living
space that some families crave. Although the popularity of under-
ground family rooms has waned, many buyers will find the idea of
using the basement for children's activities quite appealing.

Set up your Ping-Pong table (with balls and paddles as props),
hang some bright posters, dust off the old upright, and you've
instantly transformed the space into a teen hangout. Your "stage
setting" needn't be complete and shouldn't cost a cent—it's only
meant to be an imagination jogger that suggests further possibilities to buyers.

56. Highlight a workbench area.

Many men (and quite a few women, these days) dream of having a
home workshop for woodworking projects. Even if you don't
know a hammer from a jigsaw, you should clear off that dusty
workbench in your basement and draw attention to it as a sales
feature. Clean the surface, set out a few scraps of wood, a box of
nails, and a couple of tools, hang a light over the bench, and
you've set the scene for an amateur carpenter. Naturally, if someone in your family is *really* into woodworking, an honest-to-
goodness project in progress will stimulate buyers to imagine
themselves working in your pleasant basement.

Don't expect buyers to discover a selling feature like this if it is
buried under piles of boxes in a dark corner. A little detail like an
oversized workbench with a myriad of handy cubbyholes for
nails, screws, nuts, and bolts can, believe it or not, be the final
clincher that makes a buyer fall in love with your home.

Your Home's

SCREENED PORCH AND DECK

Perhaps because most buyers consider decks and screened porches to be delightful extras, these areas of a home are *big* sellers. Every house is obviously expected to have certain necessary living space—bedrooms, bathrooms, kitchen, etc.—but a well-designed deck or a charming screened porch is something of a bonus. If your home's basic interior rooms meet the buyer's expectations, a special deck or porch can be the icing on the cake, the added selling feature that convinces a buyer to choose your home over another. Make the most of these features if you are fortunate enough to have them.

57. Use plants to create indoor-outdoor transition.

Decks and porches are transitional rooms, partaking of some of the qualities of both an indoor room and the great outdoors. To make them seem a natural part of both, areas to invite the buyer from yard to home or *vice versa*, it is wise to consider a judicious use of plants. No matter how skillfully a wooden deck is designed to fit into the landscape, the structure will blend more naturally into your outdoor setting—and at the same time seem a more natural extension of your home—if you add tubs or planter boxes filled with flowers or greenery.

For instance, a tub of cascading, ruffled petunias can soften the harsh architectural lines of your deck and at the same time add a welcome spot of color. If your deck's steps are particularly wide, you might consider placing clay pots on the sides of each step and filling them with easy-to-grow geraniums. Another possibility: if you have large tubs, plant small evergreen shrubs in them, which will look handsome all year round. You need not buy out your local nursery; a few bold plantings on the deck will make a stronger, more effective statement than three dozen assorted ones.

A screened porch can feel even more like a pleasant outdoor living room with the simple addition of a few plants. Picture an old-fashioned scene of white wicker with Boston ferns, or one of sun-drenched contemporary rattán with gracefully arching *Dracaena marginata*. Or imagine hanging baskets of lush, colorful fuschia on the porch, which you can view with pleasure from inside or out. These simple spots of floral beauty can make your transitional room a unique selling aid.

58. Treat these areas as special rooms.

If you're like most owners whose homes have screened porches, you've no doubt enjoyed many pleasant hours in this relaxing setting. It should be evident that such a room can help mightily to sell your house, especially if you take a few pains to fix it up attractively. Whether you use your porch as a fresh-air living room or as a dining room, it shouldn't be furnished with mismatched Salvation Army cast-offs. Throw out that old couch with the popping springs and buy a couple of inexpensive director's chairs. If you've been making do with an ancient card table, at least cover it with an attractive cloth. Use props that will complete the inviting scene—an open seed catalog, a quilting project, a game of checkers—and enhance the lazy, summer-day mood.

But what about showing your porch to its best advantage in the middle of winter? Most people store their porch furniture inside during the cold winter months, leaving the screened porch looking empty and a bit forlorn. If you're selling in January, consider placing a few of your most weatherproof pieces of furniture back on the porch, so that buyers can imagine sitting there on a balmy afternoon. To keep the furniture safe from the elements, cover it with tarps against the most protected wall, and arrange it only when your home is going to be shown.

Your deck should be considered a room, too, and therefore merits a touch of decorating. If it is set up as an outdoor dining room, put placemats on your redwood table and open your gaily striped table umbrella. Were you planning to replace the cushions on your chairs after you settled in your new home? Why wait if bright new cushions will improve the sales appeal of your deck? Even if your deck is of modest proportions, set out a lounge chair or two and, during warm months, add a colorful beach towel, a straw hat, and a bottle of suntan lotion.

If your outdoor furniture is expensive and easily damaged by inclement weather, you won't want to keep it out on the deck during the winter months. In that case, take a hint offered earlier about displaying photographs of your home during other seasons. If the buyer can see a picture of how attractive your deck is on a rare day in June, that photograph will be worth at least the thousand words you or your realtor would have to expend in explaining the same thing. Stimulate the buyer's imagination, here as everywhere else in your home.

DRIVEWAY AND GARAGE

Rutted driveways and junk-filled garages spell Owner Neglect, and can easily sour a buyer's otherwise positive impression of your home. Give these areas an honest appraisal and see whether a few small improvements might make a world of difference. Remember that buyers are scouting for flaws, which they can use to justify a low offer. If you hope to get top dollar for your home, don't give potential buyers any extra ammunition in a poorly maintained driveway or garage.

59. Fix up driveways for first-impression impact.

Are you familiar with those amusing drawings in children's activity books, that carry the caption, "What's wrong with this picture?" Well, imagine a drawing of your home: the realty sign is up, the grass is neatly mowed, and a salesperson's car has just pulled into your driveway. So far, so good. Now a prospective buyer is stepping out of the salesperson's car—and is about to trip on that deep crack in the blacktop. Meanwhile, his wife is getting out of the other side of the car—and she's about to take a pratfall on one of your children's abandoned roller skates. Talk about making a good first impression!

The driveway is no place for children's toys—you've probably yelled yourself hoarse trying to enforce that rule. During the period that your house is on the market, skates, balls, bikes, etc., must never be left in the driveway. Not only are such things dangerous, the clutter is unsightly.

The surface of your driveway should be above reproach; after all, it's one of the first things a buyer will see when he drives up. Repair cracks and potholes, pull up pesky weeds, or get a new load of gravel. If you're selling during the winter, make sure that your driveway is clear of snow and that any icy patches are covered with sand.

60. Enlarge and improve the appearance of the garage.

A clean, organized garage appears much larger than one crammed with spare tires, fishing rods, bicycles, storm windows, lawn mowers, rakes, wheelbarrows, and two cars! Before opening your garage to the home-buying public, check out the following suggestions:

—If your garage is dark, add more lights: a bright room looks larger.

—Clear the floor by enlarging your garage's storage potential. Often this can be done with a minimum of effort and expense. Gardening tools, ladders, tennis racquets, and a myriad of other garage items can be hung from simple hooks or racks. A couple of two-by-fours nailed across the wall studs can create an instant storage bin. Overhead beams near the back of your garage can often hold large flat items like skis, fishing rods, sleds, and toboggans.

—Bicycles should be parked flat against the wall, where they will take up as little room as possible.

—If your children are incorrigible about putting away bats, balls, skates, etc., a large toy-chest catchall in the far corner of your garage will help to keep things tidy.

—If yours is a small, one-car garage, remove your car before buyers visit. An empty garage always looks larger. If yours is a two-car garage with very little extra room, remove one of your cars so that buyers can make their inspection in comfort.

Whether your property consists of fifty acres or a small suburban lot, much of the value of the package you're selling is in the land itself. Yet many sellers concentrate all of their efforts on readying their *houses* for selling, forgetting that they're also selling the acreage upon which their houses are built. If you have taken advantage of the best features of your property, if your yard is a well-landscaped setting for your home, your chances of selling quickly will be greatly enhanced.

61. Avoid an overgrown, unkempt look.

Does your yard radiate the same sense of owner pride that your home does? A lovingly maintained house that sits on a neglected piece of land has two strikes against it. So, dreary though it may be, drag out the lawn mower, sharpen up those hedge clippers, and shape up your yard:

- —Prune bushes, especially those that serve as foundation plantings. Like a good haircut, a careful clipping looks completely natural.
- —Keep your grass under control, even if it means mowing your lawn twice a week while your home is on the market. Keep grass watered through summer droughts so that it stays lushly green, and consider using sod if there is one small area of your yard where grass refuses to grow.
- —An inch or two of pine bark mulch around your foundation shrubs makes an excellent first impression (and eliminates the need to weed!).
- —Perform minor surgery if this will improve the appearance of your trees. Remove dead branches and low-hanging limbs.
- —Edge carefully where grass meets driveway or sidewalk, and check patio areas to eliminate stubborn weeds that persist in popping up between bricks or flagstones.

62. Mark your property boundaries.

Buyers want to know *exactly* what they're buying. A knowledgeable seller doesn't point vaguely in the direction of a stand of hemlocks and say, "Well, our property stops somewhere over there." No buyer will be satisfied with such inexact boundary descriptions. Unless your lot is clearly delineated by a fence or a hedge, you should define your property limits as accurately as possible.

If your boundaries are marked with surveyor's iron rods or similar obscure markings, buyers and real estate salespeople shouldn't have to go thrashing about in the undergrowth to locate them. You probably have some bamboo stakes or old wooden dowels in your basement or garage. Paint these a bright red or yellow so they'll be easy to spot, and stick them into the ground at the corners of your property. This simple little project will not only show consideration, it will be an effective sales tool.

63. Use flowering plants to dress up your yard.

If gardening is not your thing but you happen to be selling during mild seasons, brighten up your property with some flowers. Adding colorful accents to a basically green palette can divert and delight a buyer's possibly jaded eye. You don't have to be a Thalassa Cruso to create an instant mini-garden that will help to sell your home. One way is to drop by your local nursery and purchase a couple of well-established flowering plants in hanging baskets. When you get home, remove the metal hangers and plop the plants into a well-placed wheelbarrow, an old-fashioned washtub, or what have you. Such standbys as nasturtiums, petunias, impatiens, and verbena are easy to maintain if you only remember to water them regularly. Anyone can have a green thumb for the limited amount of time your home is going to be for sale. Buy a few inexpensive garden packs of blooming annuals and plant them in tight clumps for an easily attained touch of color. Try a row of sweet-smelling alyssum to line a short sidewalk or pop in some perky dwarf marigolds to form a cheerful oasis of color in your yard. In early spring, forget-me-nots will do the trick; in the fall, potted chrysanthemums will be available at most garden centers. Whatever you do, be sure to get plants that are already started and blooming, and plant close enough so that they have some collective impact.

64. Draw attention to special trees.

Many buyers can't tell an oak from an elm, but they like the notion of having a gracious, mature tree on the property they buy. If you're blessed with such a fine selling feature, make sure that it grabs the buyer's immediate attention. Hang a swing from a strong bough, slap a fresh coat of paint on an established tree-house so it won't be overlooked, move a couple of Adirondack chairs into the tree's protective shade, plant some bright, shade-tolerant flowers like impatiens or browallia around the trunk, or set up your picnic table under the tree's leafy awning.

Flowering trees will, of course, speak for themselves if they happen to be in bloom when your house is on the market. You can double their sales appeal by cutting branches of flowering crab or cherry and arranging them in vases for indoor beauty as well. Since there is no way all of your most spectacular trees or flowering bushes can be at their peak blooming periods when your home is shown, be sure to have pictures of these assets proudly displayed on your seasonal photographic board.

65. Play up flat areas.

Many yards have their ups and downs, so to speak. If yours is relatively flat, you have a potential treasure to be exploited. Even if your children have long since left the nest, it can pay off to set up your old badminton or volleyball net in that flat area of your yard. Draw prospective buyers into the scene; let them imagine their children frolicking in this ideal backyard setting. If you drag out the old croquet set, for safety's sake tie colored yarns to the wire wickets so that buyers won't trip.

By now you've mastered the art of stage setting and understand its subliminal sales message. If your mind is racing ahead with suggestions such as converting that flat lawn into a putting green or a horseshoe pitching area—fine! Just pick your props and draw positive attention to an otherwise boring (i.e., non-selling) space.

66. Set up a backyard living/dining area.

It is important to devote at least one area of your yard to outdoor living, particularly if your home doesn't have a formal deck or patio. Buyers will still recognize a scene set with picnic table and chairs and respond positively to it. At the same time, the absence of deck or patio will not be so noticeable. When selling your home during the summer months, you can set up your barbecue area to simulate a Fourth of July picnic. Cover your picnic table with a fringed, red-and-white checked cloth, set out some plastic plates (preferably blue) and glasses, bring out the barbecuing equipment, and buyers will almost smell the hot dogs cooking! In fact, though actual cooking in front of buyers is not recommended, a real charcoal fire itself has a wonderful aroma.

Consider other backyard props to set the buyer's imagination humming. A hammock stretched between two trees evokes visions of lazy summer afternoons; two old rocking chairs on a shady lawn can suggest a leisurely summertime cocktail hour.

67. Let your pool help sell your home.

If your home is being shown on a hot, sunny day, a clean swimming pool will be irresistibly inviting as well as a strong selling point in the eyes of weary, heat-beat buyers. Don't spoil the image by cluttering the water surface with a flotilla of rafts, inflatable toys, and beach balls, and be sure to store your pool cleaning paraphernalia so that buyers will not be reminded of the work involved in keeping a pool in such sparkling condition.

Since no pool is at its most appealing when hidden by its protective winter cover, consider opening your pool a month earlier or keeping it open a month later than normal if you happen to be selling at those times. Yes, keeping the filter running will increase your electric bill, but the improved appearance of your pool can help sell your home quickly, making it well worth the extra cost. Be sure to include at least one photograph of your pool at its summery best on that pictorial bulletin board, so that you can still "show it off" at times when the real thing might better serve as a skating rink.

One further fact bears emphasis here: your pool may *not* be considered an asset by some buyers. Either because they're concerned for the safety of their toddlers or because they've heard that pools require constant upkeep, some buyers are not thrilled by the prospect of owning one. Don't be discouraged if you swimming pool doesn't immediately delight every potential buyer. You can try to allay their fears by drawing up a pool-information sheet, which can be duplicated and distributed to buyers who seem sold on your home but reluctant about becoming pool owners. This sheet should include pool size, date of installation, average chemical cost per season, average cleaning/upkeep time per week, and average electric costs per season for running the filter, a well as itemizing all pool equipment that you are including in the sale. Such information can help to demystify pool ownership and turn your pool into the asset you've always considered it to be.

68. Take nighttime photographs of floodlight systems.

Let's face it, homes are rarely shown long after the sun has set, but there are some homes that look particularly lovely in the evening because of elaborate floodlighting installations. Gardens, pools, walkways, the very contours of the house itself can take on a special magic under artificial light. If you have spent a small fortune on dramatic outdoor lighting, you should suggest to your real estate agent that interested buyers schedule that ever-so-important second viewing of your home for evening hours.

The only way to stress your impressive outdoor illumination during a daytime visit is to provide appropriate photographs on your bulletin board. *Don't* take flash pictures of outdoor lighting; the effect will be completely lost. Instead, try some of the new, fast, available-light color films from Kodak with ISO speeds up to 1000. Even if your results don't fully capture the true beauty of your property, these photographs will at least pique the buyer's interest and point out a salable asset that might otherwise be overlooked.

Working with a
REAL ESTATE
AGENT

You've studied your home from attic to basement; you've spruced it up and improved its salability. Now, how do you find the right buyer? Although it's quite possible to sell your home yourself, thus saving an agent's commission, your chances of selling *quickly* are usually improved if you hire a real estate professional. A hard-working, experienced agent can save a seller countless headaches and smooth out the myriad details of selling a home. If an efficient real estate agent can sell your home quickly for a good price, it's worth paying a commission.

However, if homes in your area are selling fast and you want to take a crack at selling your home yourself, be prepared to devote a healthy chunk of time to the project. Give yourself a reasonable deadline by which to sell without an agent.

Don't skip the following section of this book just because you're considering acting as your own real estate agent. Many of the same principles apply whether you opt to employ an agent's services or not.

69. Take a Sunday drive.

Once you've fixed up your home, fight off the natural urge to reach for the phone and dial a real estate agency. Sure, you're proud of the way your home looks and you're anxious to show it off, but a few well-spent Sunday hours can make you a better-educated seller.

Real estate agencies in most parts of the country feature open houses on Sunday afternoons, when a salesperson from the agency is on duty at the house and anyone can drop in without an appointment to inspect the premises. Check your local paper and choose several such homes to tour. Read the descriptions carefully, and try to select homes that are similar to yours in size, style, and location.

While you're touring these open houses, see if you can learn anything helpful from the way they are being presented. Don't be above borrowing good ideas that may make *your* own home more salable. As you make your inspection, imagine yourself as a buyer, and notice whether the sellers have done their homework. Chances are that you'll return home quite pleased with yourself if you've already incorporated many of the tips offered in this book.

Try to compare these homes with yours and make an objective evaluation. Consider the asking prices and start thinking about what your home may be worth in comparison. Keep in mind, however, that asking prices are often much higher than final sale prices. For the time being, simply study these homes as your future competition.

One more important factor can be evaluated by visiting several open houses: you have the perfect opportunity to observe different real estate agents on the job. Note how effectively each open house is organized. Are there attractive signs outside the home? Are there printed listing forms available inside the home that detail essential specifications? Is the agent on duty helpful without being too pushy? As you leave each house, you may want to inform the agent that you are planning to put your own home on the market. If you do, note which agents follow up with a phone call. That's the kind of eager professionalism you should expect in the agent who handles the eventual sale of your home.

70. Ask friends and neighbors for personal recommendations.

Too many ill-informed sellers literally let their fingers do the walking—they pick up the phone book, turn to the yellow pages, and contact the real estate agency whose advertisement is the largest or flashiest. Is this how you'd choose a family doctor or lawyer? Of course not; you'd ask for referrals.

If any of your friends have moved from your area during the past year, they're the perfect people to seek out for advice. Ask them which agency they used, who the listing agent was, if they were satisfied with the service they received, and if they would use the same agency again. Ask for an open, honest evaluation of the real estate agency that handled the sale of their home, and take notes as you listen.

Your next step should be to speak with neighbors who have recently bought in your neighborhood. Ask them the same type of

questions and see who they recommend. By now your list of
agencies may be getting quite long, and you may be becoming
more and more confused. Before you shrug and make a selection
by the "eenie-meanie-minie-moe" method, realize that your
choice of an agency is of great importance. It can make the
difference between a fast, fair, painless sale and one that drags on
interminably only to fall apart months later.

71. Interview at least three agents.

When you have narrowed your list of real estate agencies to a
manageable number, call each of them and ask to speak to the
salesperson who was recommended by your friends and neighbors. Don't assume that all agents in an office are equally efficient; if a particular agent has been touted by your friends as
being an excellent salesperson, that's the one you want to deal
with as your listing agent.

Why is a listing agent important? If you select an enthusiastic,
professional agent, that person will handle your listing conscien-
tiously, making sure that your home receives sufficient advertising and maximum exposure. A lazy, disorganized listing agent,
even one who works for the top agency in town, can prove to be a
decided detriment to selling your home.

Don't be in a hurry to give your home's listing to the first agent
who walks through your front door and immediately starts gush-
ing about how "charming" your home is and how he or she has
the "perfect buyers." Make the competing agents *earn* your
listing. After all, they'll be handling a transaction involving many
thousands of dollars. *Your* dollars!

Sit down with each agent over a cup of coffee, after showing
your home. Before the agent begins his or her pitch for obtaining
your listing, take the initiative and interview the agent. Remember, *you're* doing the hiring.

Be sure to include the following questions when interviewing
each agent:

—"How long have you been selling real estate? Full-time or
part-time?" A full-time veteran of ten years has a proven
track record, yet don't discount a relative newcomer who
may make up in enthusiasm what he or she lacks in experience—especially if the bright beginner has the services of a
top agency as backup. Be on your guard against listing with
a part-time dilettante who merely dabbles in real estate

three hours a week. Your listing won't get the time and attention it deserves.

—"How large is your firm? How many full-time salespeople are employed?" The large real estate agency often has a bigger advertising budget and gets more referrals from out-of-state agencies, particularly if the office is affiliated with a national chain. An efficient small agency, on the other hand, often gives more personal attention to individual listings. To sell quickly, avoid the one-horse agency that operates without the necessary staff.

—"Why is your agency the right one to handle the sale of our home?" An enthusiastic listing agent should display both eagerness and pride in the firm for which he or she works. Top agencies keep their fingers on the pulse of the housing industry and help their salespeople stay up to date on mortgage trends and price fluctuations.

—"If you were to write an ad for our home, what features would you emphasize in the selling copy?" This is an excellent way to test an agent for originality. If the agent mentions the obvious—"four-bedroom ranch in nice neighborhood"—chances are good that this person lacks the qualities of creative salesmanship. In times of high mortgage rates and slow-moving house sales, a listing agent must develop a creative sales approach in order to have a competitive edge. Search out that individual who will respond intuitively to the salable features of your home.

72. Decide upon the type of listing you want.

Every agent you interview will ask that you list your home exclusively with his or her firm. Before you sign a listing contract, you should understand some of the different types of listings so that you can choose the one that is best for you.

An **exclusive right-to-sell listing** is an agreement that you make with one agency entitling you to that agency's best services. The agency should advertise your home, hold open house, and enter your home's listing in the computerized multiple listing service in your area. In return, you agree to pay the agency a commission if your house sells within the contract period—even if you happen to locate the buyer yourself. An active multiple listing service can give your home maximum exposure, so be sure that the agency to which you assign an exclusive right-to-sell is a member. Once your listing agent has entered your home in the multiple listing service, member agencies will also be working to sell your home. You pay only one commission if your house sells—to the listing agency. If a member agency has sold your home, the two agencies then split the commission.

An **exclusive agency listing** differs from the exclusive right-to-sell listing in that you retain the right to locate and sell to a buyer without being obliged to pay a commission to the agency.

An **open listing** is a nonexclusive listing. You can give an open listing to several agencies at the same time, but only the agency that succeeds in selling your home receives a commission. You reserve the right to sell to a buyer whom you locate without owing any agency a commission. The main drawback to an open listing is that the agencies are not obligated to advertise your home. On the other hand, you have the advantage of having several agencies out there hustling to sell your home in the expectation of earning a full commission.

Sometimes a seller will give an open listing to several agencies for a limited time period (two to four weeks) with the understanding that he will later award an exclusive listing to the agency of his choice if the home hasn't sold at the end of that period. This technique certainly inspires agents to work their tails off, but all of this activity can be a little deceiving. There are agencies that will blitz your house with prospective buyers in an effort to impress you. Unfortunately, you have no means of knowing whether these customers are financially qualified to buy your home or merely bodies dragged through your home to make the agency or listing agent look good.

Follow your educated instincts. If one agent stands out from the rest and you are impressed with his or her integrity and the shining reputation of his or her agency, you should feel safe signing an exclusive with that agency. Sign for a reasonable period of time so that the agency can publicize your home and work on selling it for at least two months. Never sign for a period longer than three months; after that length of time, you should have the option of trying another agency if you are disappointed in your first agency's performance. Before signing the listing agreement, read all the small print and be sure you understand what you are signing. If anything worries you, consult your lawyer before signing.

73. Realize that commission rates are negotiable.

Contrary to popular opinion, real estate commission rates are not carved in stone. Legally, real estate agencies cannot band together to set fixed commission rates. You will find, however, that there is little variation in the rates that agencies ask. Six or seven percent is common in most areas.

When you list with an agency, you *can* negotiate for a lower commission, but accept the fact that you may not get the full services of the agency at that lower rate. If yours is a very salable home and houses in your area are selling quickly, it's much more likely that requesting a lower commission will work to your advantage.

In tight real estate markets, however, your chances of selling quickly are probably improved if you agree to pay the going rate of commission. Salespeople may hustle just that little bit extra for a higher commission, and the agency will not begrudge giving your listing a fair advertising budget.

A commission rate can sometimes be renegotiated when an offer is presented. If your agent conveys an offer that is close to what you'll accept but not quite high enough, and the buyer refuses to come up to your price, you've got a stalemate situation. Rather than lose the sale, your agent may agree to cut the commission in order to give you your price. But don't expect this concession as a matter of course, and don't suggest it as a solution every time you receive an offer that is too low. If your agent has been working hard for you, he or she deserves to be fairly compensated.

74. Insist upon at least one open house.

If you choose to give an exclusive listing to an agency, that agency must work hard for you, and it's up to you to demand that they do so. Before signing a listing agreement, explain to your listing agent that you expect the agency to hold at least one open house within the first two weeks of the listing contract period. This open house, if well publicized, should bring out both buyers and other interested real estate agents.

Some agencies are lazy and think open houses are a colossal waste of time. This is a foolish notion. Yes, there will be lots of "just lookings," who have nothing better to do on a Sunday afternoon, but a well-advertised open house can also draw serious buyers, or even nosy neighbors who happen to have friends who would love to move into your area.

It's a smart idea to write an agreement to hold an open house right into your listing contract before you sign. This indicates to the listing agent that you are an educated seller who understands his rights.

75. Obtain a written agreement on advertising your home.

Agencies can promise you the moon, but unless you have it in writing, you may never live to see those promises become realities. If you sign an exclusive right-to-sell listing agreement with an agency, they should be obligated to advertise frequently until your home is sold or the listing contract expires. Since advertising is expensive and many agencies work within tight advertising budgets, you should get a written agreement stipulating how often the agency will advertise your home and in what publications they intend to advertise.

Generally speaking, higher-priced homes deserve to receive a larger advertising budget. If your agency stands to earn a $10,000 commission on the sale of your home, they can afford to be generous with their advertising budget. On the other hand, if an agency's total commission will be $3,000, don't expect them to spend $1,000 advertising your home in *Town & Country*.

Be sure your agency doesn't bypass advertising in your town's local paper(s). This initial ad with a photograph of your home may serve to notify some unknown person across town that your home, which she has always coveted, is now available.

Naturally, you should expect to receive copies of all the ads for your home from your listing agent as they are published. If you don't think the advertising copy is effective, don't be afraid to say so. Remember, you've hired *them* to work for you.

76. Request a weekly progress report from your listing agent.

Sometimes agents take your listing, show your home, and never communicate until they have a sound offer. After going through all the trouble of making your home as salable as possible and selecting a real estate professional, are you willing to sit back and wait for an offer? You shouldn't be! You needn't make a pest of yourself calling your listing agent every other day, but you should stay on top of things by demanding to be kept informed.

An efficient listing agent will call you to report buyers' reactions to your home, even if those reactions are negative. Listen to the comments and see if you can correct the problems those buyers reported. Don't make the mistake of wrapping yourself up in a cozy cocoon and thinking your house is perfect. No house is perfect. Be open to making small changes in yours that could impress the *next* prospective buyers.

From time to time you should meet with your listing agent and have a strategy meeting. Feel free to offer suggestions for selling or advertising your home more effectively and more quickly. Be flexible and be willing to change your plan of attack. The seller who lies back in his hammock and waits for the agent to sell his home can get lost in the shuffle.

77. Review the listing form to be sure all information is correct.

Once your agent has drawn up a listing form for your home, review it diligently or you can expect trouble further down the line. This listing information is the detailed data that salespeople will give to prospective buyers. It must be perfect and error free.

An agency's listing form should include every item that is to be sold with the house (e.g., wall-to-wall carpeting, storm windows, screens, TV antenna, appliances, etc.). Everything should be spelled out at this stage so that you avoid ugly battles later on with buyers who "assumed" that your draperies were included in the sales price. List all appliances to be included, and specifically mention items that are not to be included in the sale (e.g., your grandmother's crystal chandelier in the dining room, your new freezer in the basement, etc.).

Many a sale has fallen through at the last moment because these details were not written into the original listing form. Go over every item with your agent and be sure that you have clarified any questionable item. If you wish, you can draw up a list of items that you are willing to sell to the new owners over and above the sales price.

78. Arrive at an equitable asking price.

How do you determine what your home is worth? Most sellers are simply too emotionally involved to be able to set a fair price on their own homes. Setting a price has to be one of the most difficult problems encountered in selling your home.

Basically, your home is worth the top price that someone is willing to pay for it at the time you're selling it. During rough real estate times, such as we've experienced in recent years, your home may fetch less than you estimate its worth to be. On the other hand, you may be lucky even during a recession and find a buyer who falls in love with your home and is willing to pay *any* price to own it. How then does one arrive at an asking price?

You should ask each agent whom you interview to work up a market value analysis. There should be no charge for this service. Any agent who is interested in obtaining your listing should be willing to do the required homework. This market analysis should compare your home with *recent sales* of comparable homes in your area. The fairest method of pricing your home would be to compare it with an exact duplicate that sold yesterday. Since no two homes are exactly alike, a market analysis will compare your home with at least three homes that are similar to yours. The agent should be aware of any unusual sales conditions that may have affected the final sales prices of those homes. For instance, if a home is sold in a hurry to pay off debts, the price may be lower than market value. If a home is sold with heavy owner financing, the price may be higher than market value. Final sales figures should be used, never asking prices. Your neighbors may have asked $10,000 more than they finally received, but don't depend on them to report an honest sales price to you. Some sellers simply love to inflate their sales prices to make you green with envy.

If your house is very similar to others that have sold recently in your neighborhood, it's fairly easy to establish an equitable asking price. It's much harder to determine a price for an unusual home that has few comparable examples. For instance, in some parts of the country, old homes are at a premium regardless of their condition. It's simply a case of demand exceeding supply. In some areas, extremely modern homes are difficult to sell and often go for lower prices than you might expect.

Study the market value reports that the agencies have drawn

up and try to set your home's price where it logically seems to fall, not where you *want* it to be. In the final analysis, *you* set your price—your agent can only suggest a price.

Beware the agent who suggests an inflated price for your home. This is a common ploy to obtain your listing. In order to butter up the buyer and obtain an exclusive listing, an unscrupulous agent may list your home for an exorbitant price. After a while, you can be sure that same agent will suggest that you lower your price because of a tight mortgage market, a slow selling season, or some other excuse. Meanwhile, you've lost precious selling time.

Once you've established what you consider to be a fair sales price, it's wise to add a few thousand dollars as bargaining leeway. This is tricky. Add too much and your home sounds so overpriced that no one will bother to look at it. Add too little and you'll be fielding ridiculously low offers. The safest rule of thumb is to add between five and ten percent to form your asking price. Try out this figure on your agent and listen to his advice. Remember that no agency will work hard on an overpriced listing. Be reasonable.

In determining your asking price, you've probably tossed around a bottom-line figure in your mind, that price under which you positively will not sell. Don't feed this information to your agent. Once you've set a price, never refer to this figure as your asking price. Expect your agent to bring in an offer close to your listing price. If your agent knows how low you will go, your chances of getting a high price are reduced.

If you're still nervous about setting your price, pay to have an independent appraiser give you an estimate of your home's value. The fee for this service is usually under two hundred dollars, and having this information may make you feel more secure in determining your price and setting your own bottom line.

When Your
HOME IS SHOWN

Of course, like all home sellers, you're fantasizing that the first prospective buyers who walk through your front door will fall madly in love with your home and offer to meet your price right then and there. That's every seller's dream. It can happen, but it's a rare occurrence.

By now, your home is in peak sales condition, you've employed a top-notch real estate agency, and your property is priced realistically. These three factors should make your home sell quickly and give you a distinct selling edge over your neighbor, whose home has been on the market for five long months. Before you start resting on your laurels, however, study the following set of guidelines, which every seller should adhere to when his house is on the market.

79. Be willing to show your home (practically) any time.

Play the odds. The more people who see your home, the more likely you are to sell it quickly. Yes, it's an inconvenience to show your home at dinnertime, but if the people buy your home, isn't it worth a reheated pot roast?

Many sellers set difficult restrictions on showing their houses, forcing agents to schedule appointments at least twenty-four hours in advance and only between certain hours. Try to be more flexible so that you don't lose prospective buyers. Don't adopt the attitude that serious buyers will wait to see your home at *your* convenience; those same buyers may end up buying your neighbor's home because you didn't want to miss your favorite soap opera. Unless you're having a party or someone in your home is seriously ill, bend over backwards to make your home available for showing.

If you're frequently away from home during the day, or if you plan to spend a few days out of town, trust your agent with the key to your home. If you are nervous about having unfamiliar sales-people taking strangers through your home in your absence, you can stipulate that your listing agent must accompany any other salesperson. Of course, you should never leave valuable jewelry or large sums of cash lying around any time your home is shown —that's only asking for trouble.

80. Have a family "game plan" for last-minute showings.

It's nine o'clock on a Saturday morning, the house is a mess, and the telephone rings. No, you haven't won the Irish Sweepstakes, it's your cheerful real estate agent asking if she can show your home in twenty minutes!

Don't push the proverbial panic button. Prepare for these inevitable, unexpected last-minute showings by formulating a family game plan. To be effective, this plan should be worked out by all your family and actually written down on a chart, so that everyone in your household knows exactly what to do if you sound the alarm.

No one is talking major housecleaning at this point. The kinds of tasks you ought to be concerned with now are simple ones: dust the dining table top if you can write your name on it; stuff last night's dirty lasagna pan into the dishwasher; hide those damp pantyhose hanging on the shower rod. Even young children can participate by "cleaning" their rooms (i.e., tossing everything into those wonderful underbed catchalls). If you keep a sense of humor, this last-minute rush may seem like a speeded up old-time movie with people running off in all directions to make your home presentable. As long as your family understands the game plan, you'll be surprised how effectively you can neaten up your home for these ill-timed showings.

Don't be a perfectionist. Do the best you can within your deadline, then relax when the doorbell rings. And don't you dare apologize about the condition of your home! That's starting the buyers out on a negative note.

81. Air out your home half an hour before showing.

Any home will smell better if you open windows in each room and let some fresh air in. Even during colder months, you should consider airing out your home before buyers come to inspect it. Stale air isn't appealing, particularly in a home with smokers or pets.

We become so accustomed to the odors in our homes that it's easy to ignore them, but buyers, coming in from the outdoors, will be responsive to any smells that aren't fresh and clean. Air-conditioned homes should also be aired out, so that there are no lingering odors.

Finally, on a bright, warm spring day, leave all your windows open if the temperature within your home is pleasant. There's something so appealing about fresh-smelling rooms, wide-open windows, and a gentle breeze ruffling your curtains.

82. Set your thermostat at a comfortable temperature.

Yes, we all want to save on our heating costs, and budget-conscious people turn down their thermostats and throw on an extra sweater. But a chilly house can make buyers nervous and set them to wondering if your home is poorly insulated or your furnace is on its last legs.

When you know that prospective buyers are on their way, push up your thermostat and shed your long-johns. This is not the time to economize. You want the buyers to feel comfortable as they tour your home.

Naturally, the same rule applies during the summer months. If your home is air conditioned and the temperature outside is a sweltering ninety-five degrees, cool off your house to show buyers how effectively your central air conditioning works.

83. Turn on lights in each and every room.

Real estate salespeople can't be expected to remember where every light switch in your home is located. You can make home showings smoother for your agent if you turn on lights in every room before prospective buyers arrive. This also gives you the opportunity to select the lighting effects you want for each room. Be sure not to overlook areas like your attic and basement where light switches are often difficult to locate. Each bathroom and closet should also have a light turned on.

Don't begrudge your electric company a few more dollars on this month's bill if extra lighting can make your home seem cheerful on a dreary day. No area of your home should appear dark or depressing, so unless a room is bathed in sunlight, turn on those lights and brighten up your home's sales appeal.

84. Turn on pleasant background music.

Music has subliminal powers. Why else would stores bother to pipe in soft background music if not to put customers in a comfortable, relaxed mood for—what else—buying? Let music add to the special ambience of your home. Imagine the gentle strains of Vivaldi's "Four Seasons" in your sun-drenched breakfast room or the mellow jazz of George Shearing in your cozy den. But whatever you play, keep it quiet and unobtrusive, with the volume turned down to the just audible level.

Avoid playing music that jars the senses. Rock is taboo, as is anything with a thumping base. Your selections should be soothing and pleasant to the ear. Also, avoid vocal music. If a buyer is straining to catch the lyrics, chances are he won't be paying attention to the main attraction, namely your home.

Speaking of sound, every seller should know better than to leave a television set blaring away when his home is being shown. This is rude and distracting. A sitcom's raucous laugh track is hardly pleasant background "music" for house selling.

85. Put pets out and send children to play at the neighbors'.

Your friendly, tail-wagging, loud-barking Rover should *not* be the family member who greets prospective buyers at the door. As adorable as you may think he is, don't expect all buyers to appreciate his unchecked exuberance. Bear in mind that some visitors may be terrified of dogs or cats or suffer from allergic responses to your animals. So, tie up Rover and banish Morris to the basement while you home is being shown.

Perhaps it's unfair to lump children with pets, but kids can cause just as much trouble when you're trying to sell a house. That precious toddler can turn into a cranky little monster the minute buyers step across the threshold. At least dogs can't talk. Children can, and oh, what things they say! If you don't want buyers to know that you're selling your house because the poltergeist in the playroom is driving you bonkers, shoo your kids out to play at a neighbor's and let buyers inspect your home in peace.

86. Keep out of sight when a salesperson is showing your home.

Once you've answered the door and welcomed the real estate agent and potential buyers, you should find something else to do—preferably outside of your home. This is the time to take a walk or visit your neighbors or go grocery shopping.

It's a fact that no buyer feels completely comfortable viewing a house if the seller is hovering anxiously in the wings. In an ideal selling situation, buyers should feel free to discuss a home with their agent without worrying about offending the owner.

One added benefit of having the owners vacate a home while it is being shown is that buyers can more easily imagine the house as their own. The shrewd seller sets the scene so that buyers can walk onto the stage and immediately begin play-acting, pretending the home is already theirs.

87. Never volunteer information.

It's human nature to brag about your home and your neighborhood to prospective buyers—after all, you know your home better than the salesperson who is showing it. True enough, but your salesperson knows the buyers better than you do, knows what they're looking for, and knows what aspects of your home will appeal to their particular needs.

If you've followed the previous tip, you won't be around to chat up the buyers, but if you *are* at home, resist the urge to volunteer information about what you consider to be important sales features. It's all too easy to develop seller's foot-in-mouth disease. You hear yourself saying, "This block's school bus stop is right in front of our house," and then learn the prospective buyers have no children, work the evening shift, and love to sleep late in the morning! Or you babble on and on about the friendliness of your neighborhood, the weekly summer barbecues, the winter bridge tournaments—only to learn that the prospective buyers are loners who want no part of forced community activities.

On the other hand, don't feel compelled to apologize for what you see as your home's selling weaknesses. You may be moving because you can't tolerate the traffic noise from the newly built expressway one block away, yet prospective buyers moving from a city setting may not have even noticed the noise level until you pointed it out. In fact, your home may have seemed perfect to them because of the very proximity of the expressway for quick commuting. But the moment a seller apologizes, a buyer naturally becomes wary.

Be smart: let the salesperson do the job of selling.

88. Consider buyer amenities.

Although a buyer's visit to your home should be treated as a business appointment rather than a social engagement, there are a few niceties that can make the experience more pleasant for the weary house-hunter. In the cold of winter, for instance, buyers might enjoy a steaming cup of coffee, or, on a hot summer day, a tall glass of lemonade or iced tea. There's no need to overdo it with homemade donuts or Grandma's prize coffee cake; keep it simple and informal. And remember to do your disappearing act as soon as your visitors have been served!

If you're among the growing number of families that don't allow smoking in the home, consider relaxing your rule while your house is on the market. As offensive as smoking may be to you personally, you do want buyers to be at ease when touring your home. Smokers will appreciate your thoughtfulness if you provide ashtrays in most rooms—and you'll spare your carpet from fallen ashes.

As mentioned before, provide extra hangers in the coat closet in case buyers want to shed their wraps, and set out clean towels and fresh soap in the bathrooms. Thoughtful touches like these will make buyers feel at home.

89. Draw up a floor plan.

A simple floor plan of your home can be an effective selling tool, a "visual aid" that will help buyers to remember your house after they leave. Since buyers usually see several homes in a day of house hunting, they often have difficulty recalling particular layouts. You can be one up on your competition if you have taken the time to draw up a floor plan of each level of your home and provide copies for all interested buyers.

You don't need a degree in architecture to draw up a rudimentary floor plan. Simply buy some blue-ruled grid paper at any stationery store, measure the dimensions of your rooms, and draw a rough layout of your rooms on the grid paper. When you have the sketches Xeroxed, the printed blue lines usually disappear from your copies, and your floor plan will look quite professional.

Leave these floor plans in a convenient place—on your hall table, for instance—and be sure salespeople know where to find them, since it will be up to them to hand them out. When prospective buyers take home your floor plan, they can continue the game of imagining themselves living in your house by arranging their furniture in your rooms.

90. Assemble house records for buyer perusal.

In these times of rising energy costs, buyers will most certainly ask what your home heating and electric costs are. Be prepared by having your records organized in a handy file. Break down your housing costs by month, so that buyers can see at a glance what their expenses would be. It's a good idea to include copies of your paid utility bills to back up the figures on your monthly payment chart.

Your real estate tax information also belongs in this house records file along with any other miscellaneous figures such as garbage collection fees, sewer assessments, etc. If you break down the large yearly figures into a monthly budget, prospective buyers won't be so overwhelmed by the numbers.

If you are including any appliances in the sales price of your home, you should keep warranties and instruction booklets in this same file. And, of course, salespeople should be thoroughly familiar with the file and its contents, since they will most often be called upon to answer questions. Be professional by having the answers to buyers' questions available at a moment's notice, all neatly assembled in one ready file of information.

91. Provide a map of your area.

All prospective buyers, particularly those new to your area, will be concerned about the location of essential services in relationship to your home. A considerate (and clever) seller will have anticipated the buyers' questions, and will have prepared a map of the area surrounding his home.

You can usually procure a town map through your local chamber of commerce. If a printed map is not available, it's easy enough to draw up your own simplified map of your area. Mark the location of your home in red and be sure to indicate such features as:

—schools
—stores
—laundromats and dry cleaners
—churches and synagogues
—bus routes
—parks and playgrounds
—libraries
—movie theaters
—restaurants
—hospitals
—gas stations

Be sure to make plenty of copies for your agent to hand out. This simple, thoughtful favor will be appreciated by any buyer who is considering your home.

92. Tell everyone you meet that your house is for sale.

Why keep it a secret? If you're interested in selling quickly and painlessly, you should let everyone and anyone know that your house is available. Your neighbors across the street may have friends who have been wanting to move into the neighborhood. Your family pediatrician may know of a new doctor who's moving into your town and wants to buy a home like yours because it's near the hospital. Your local librarian may have a house-hunting friend who has admired your home for years. Word of mouth is a strong selling aid. If each person you tell that your house is for sale tells two more people, and those people each tell two more people, and so forth, the good word can spread quite rapidly. Verbal advertising is free; put it to work for you.

93. Remain optimistic.

It's easy to get discouraged after your house has been shown ten or twelve times and no offer is forthcoming. You've done everything to make your wonderful home more salable, and yet it seems that no one appreciates it. If this happens, don't take buyers' rejections personally. Remember that the right buyers will come along; it's just a matter of time.

Keep in touch with your listing agent and ask for feedback from prospective buyers who have viewed your home. If you learn that Couple One thought it was too small for their large family and Couple Two thought it was located too far from their office, you'll feel better knowing the reasons why those buyers didn't make an offer were things over which you had no control.

Keep reminding yourself that one of these days (and it could happen tomorrow) someone is going to walk through your front door and fall head over heels in love with your home. After all, you did! There is surely a buyer out there who will respond to the same unique set of qualities that attracted you to your home in the first place.

GET AN OFFER

This homestretch of the selling process can really test your mettle. Keep your cool, and don't let dollar signs blind you into accepting the highest offer without understanding the fine print in the contract. After you've read the following final tips, you'll know why a slightly lower offer can sometimes be a better deal for you. And you'll also know how to stay calm and collected as you and your agent negotiate the most advantageous—and the fastest—sale of your home.

94. Consider only written offers.

If a salesperson calls to tell you that his customers are "thinking" of offering you, say, $70,000, this is not a legal offer but merely a fishing expedition. The agent and prospective buyers are testing the waters, so to speak, to feel you out on how low a price you might be willing to accept. Don't play their game. You're under no obligation to respond to this verbal offer. In fact, if you agree to $70,000 over the phone, chances are that these same buyers will try to shave off a few more thousand from your price when and if (and that's a big "if") they finally get around to making you a written offer, which is the only kind that counts.

Insist that every offer be in writing, signed by the prospective buyers. This is the only professional way of doing business.

95. Don't be afraid to accept your first offer.

If you've done your homework (no pun intended), it may be that your home is now so irresistible that you receive an offer of only $500 under the listing price the very first week it's for sale. Lucky you! But instead of rejoicing over their good fortune, many sellers panic, suspecting that if a house sells that quickly, it must be underpriced. Foolishly, they reject the offer and increase their asking price by $10,000—only to find themselves sitting on an unsold house six months later.

If you are fortunate enough to receive a first offer that is very close to your listing price, it means that the prospective buyers appreciate your home and want it badly. You can take a gamble and reject their first offer in the hope that they will turn around and pay your full price, but why risk losing such an effortless sale?

Don't forget that every buyer wants to feel that he has got a "deal"—that's one reason why you built bargaining leeway into your price in the first place. If you start holding out for your full asking price at this stage of the game, you may well offend the buyer who made you a very fair offer, and you may lose this buyer forever. If the terms of the sale are attractive and the offer close to your asking price, it's time to pop the cork and start celebrating!

96. Never reject a low offer without making a counteroffer.

When a buyer makes an insultingly low offer for your home, you're tempted to tell him to buzz off and never darken your doorstep again. Instead, restrain your baser instincts and try not to take his offending offer personally. That prospective buyer has picked up some questionable advice along the line: he thinks the only way to barter to a fair price is to start very low. Unfortunately, in this game of house buying, there are very few formal rules to guide the players' conduct. There are buyers who thrive on the challenge of negotiating, who wouldn't pay full price for a lifejacket if they were on the *Titanic*. And there are other buyers who hate the bargaining process, who will make their best offer only once and then retire from the arena.

As a home seller, you're obligated to play the game—but you're entitled to set your own rules. Just try not to be inflexible. If your listing price is $80,000 and someone offers you $70,000, you can counteroffer at $79,500! A counteroffer should let buyers know that you are willing to negotiate, but not in the bargain basement.

Negotiating can take many forms. You can counteroffer by lowering your price slightly and excluding some appliances from the sale, or you can stick by your original price but throw in some extras like a lawn mower and garden tractor. Counteroffers keep the ball in play and, to mix a metaphor, keep the prospective buyer on the hook.

97. Avoid accepting an offer loaded with contingency clauses.

There is much more to an offer than the price alone. You've got to study each one carefully to see what contingencies the buyers are attaching to their financial offer. Generally speaking, the strongest offer contains the fewest contingency clauses. These extra stipulations in an offer are, in fact, buyer escape hatches that can make your sale weak and nonbinding.

Unless a buyer is planning to pay all cash for your home, he will include a financing clause stipulating that his offer is contingent upon his receiving a mortgage. Some buyers will insert a clause specifying that an offer is contingent upon your home passing certain inspections by contractors and exterminators. These are normal and generally acceptable contingency clauses.

The red flag to watch for in an offer is a statement that makes a buyer's offer contingent upon his selling his home. His offer requires you to take your home off the market while he tries to sell his. Do you need to participate in this game of "musical houses"?

If you're selling in a sellers' market (i.e., mortgage money is plentiful and affordable, there are more buyers than sellers, and houses are selling like hotcakes), you don't need to tie yourself down to such a dubious sale. You can probably afford to wait for a buyer who is free and clear to buy your home without such contingencies.

When home sales are more difficult because of high interest rates, a seller may consider accepting such an offer if he feels that the buyer is sincere. If you accept such a contingency offer because the market is poor, you must protect yourself by taking the following measures:

—Give the buyer a limited time period in which to sell his house. One month is standard.
—Call the agency that has listed your buyer's house. Ask the listing agent if it is priced fairly and whether it is highly salable. Don't let the sale of your home depend on the unrealistic expectations that your buyer has for selling his present home.
—Keep your house on the market and insist that your agency continue to show it. If you receive another acceptable offer for your home (an offer without such a sales restriction), the original buyer has twenty-four hours to remove his

contingency clause or his offer is null and void. This arrangement should be written into any agreement.

—Never consider that your home is sold under these circumstances. You can't depend on selling to a buyer who is not free to buy.

98. Specify a time limit for a buyer to obtain a mortgage.

As mentioned earlier, the best offer is one with the fewest contingencies. If you have to deal with contingencies, it's to your advantage as a seller to set time limits on any of them so that you will have a solid, contingency-free contract of sale as quickly as possible. Your agent—who should be working to protect your interests—should write a deadline into any offer to give the buyers a fair but limited amount of time in which to obtain a mortgage commitment. Seven to ten days' time is usually a reasonable limit to impose.

If you sign an offer that sets no time limit on the mortgage contingency clause, buyers can then shop around for weeks looking for the best mortgage rates while you nervously twiddle your thumbs, knowing that your sale is shaky until this contingency is removed from the contract.

During times of high mortgage rates, buyers may turn to you and ask for some degree of owner financing if they strike out at the banks. *Never* agree to this arrangement unless you've consulted both your lawyer and your accountant. If they advise you to consider helping with the financing in order to sell your home, the buyers should realize that you are making a big concession; under these conditions, you should expect to receive top dollar for your home in return for your providing some financial assistance.

99. Insist upon a substantial deposit.

An offer should be accompanied by a deposit—so-called "earnest money" which proves that a buyer is putting his money where his mouth is. Customs vary throughout the country in regard to the amount of down payment that a buyer is expected to make. Generally speaking, no home should be taken off the market—which is what you're doing when you accept an offer—without the buyer depositing at least $500 in escrow with the agent or lawyer as third party to the sale. In many parts of the country, one percent of the sale price is expected from the buyers at the time they sign a binder and ten percent at the time of signing a contract. Whatever the customs in your area, don't consider signing an offer that is accompanied by a mere token deposit. The buyer is risking next to nothing, and may be signaling that he is in no way financially qualified to buy your home.

100. Be sure your buyer is financially qualified.

Before you accept an offer and take your home off the market, you should feel relatively secure that the buyer can afford to follow through on the sale. Particularly during times of high interest rates, buyers need large incomes to qualify for mortgage loans, and banks may require substantial downpayments. A good real estate agent not only keeps abreast of local financing requirements, but makes sure that buyers are financially qualified even before showing them any properties.

The salesperson who is presenting an offer should have financial background information on anyone who is interested in purchasing your home. Don't be shy about requesting this information. You have every right to know how sound a buyer's finances are before tying yourself into a deal. A marginally qualified buyer whose wants exceed his wallet can cause you to lose a couple of weeks of valuable selling time while he searches in vain for a mortgage commitment.

101. Seek legal advice.

The offer looks good and your real estate agent is pressing for your John Hancock on the dotted line. Stop! Don't let the excitement of the moment overwhelm your better judgment.

What is it that you're about to sign? In your area of the country, offers may be made in the form of a binder—a written agreement drawn up by a real estate agent to serve only until the formal sales contract is drawn up by a lawyer. If you choose to sign a binder, protect yourself by adding the written stipulation that your acceptance of the offer is contingent upon your lawyer's approval of the document.

If the offer is being presented as a formal sales contract, never sign until your lawyer reviews the terms and conditions so that your best interests are protected. It will be well worth the legal fee if his advice prevents you from making a mistake that could drag out the whole selling process for additional weeks. After all, the whole point of this book has been to make your home sell faster.

Having reviewed the offer with your lawyer and having obtained his confirmation that the offer is sound and solid, you can afford to congratulate yourself on a job well done. Your efforts have paid off and it's time to bask in the pleasant shade of that sign on your front lawn—the one that says SOLD!